Advance Praise for *Change of Heart*

"*Change of Heart* is a tragic story of senseless violence, horrific loss, and, in the end, forgiveness that is astonishing. I kept asking myself, 'As a Christian, could I be as strong and merciful as Jeanne Bishop?' I have my doubts."

—Best-selling author John Grisham

"*Change of Heart* is a powerful story of faith, forgiveness, and reconciliation. This is a painfully honest account of a remarkable and courageous journey from the tragedy and pain of the murder of family members to a place of freedom and grace."

—Maurice Possley, Pulitzer Prize-winning
journalist and author

"A person is more than the worst thing he or she has ever done. God loves all human beings and endows them with dignity and worth. Juvenile life without parole sentences tell people who committed their crimes as juveniles that they are human garbage, to be thrown away into the maw of prison until the day they die. The criminal justice system in the United States, which deems some people unworthy of redemption—even children who commit serious crimes—urgently needs to hear voices that speak for mercy and restoration. Jeanne Bishop's is such a voice."

—Sister Helen Prejean, activist and
author of *Dead Man Walking*

"There is a lot of grace in Jeanne Bishop's elegant, elegiac book *Change of Heart,* but it is not a wimpy hearts-and-flowers kind of grace. Instead, it is a heartfelt, gut-wrenching kind of grace. Powerful grace. Transformative grace. This is an utterly surprising story of redemption. It is an unflinching look at the very real cost of blessing—truly blessing—someone else. Jeanne's story of restorative justice haunts me. The stunning letter she wrote to her sister's murderer still lingers. And the story of the grace of the gift of two quarters is one I will retell and retell again. *Change of heart* is what happens when someone, in the depths of despair, cries, 'This is too much for me. God, take it and redeem it,' and believes . . . no matter the cost. Please read this book."

—Robert Darden, Associate Professor of
Journalism, Public Relations and New Media
at Baylor University and author of *Nothing but Love
in God's Water: Black Sacred Music from the Civil War
to the Civil Rights Movement, Volume I*

"Jeanne Bishop's words have the power to heal the hearts of the grieving, convict the hearts of the judgmental, and liberate the hearts of a nation hardened by fear, vengeance, and excessive punishment. *Change of Heart* is a must-read for pastors, social workers, caregivers, and all who seek to build community with people relegated to the margins."

—Greg Ellison, Assistant Professor of Pastoral Care
and Counseling, Emory University, and
author of *Cut Dead but Still Alive: Caring
for African American Young Men*

"When I commuted the death sentences of everyone on Illinois's death row, I expressed the hope that we could open our hearts and provide something for victims' families other than the hope of revenge. I quoted Abraham Lincoln: 'I have always found that mercy bears richer fruits than strict justice.' Jeanne Bishop's compelling book tells the story of how devotion to her faith took her face-to-face with her sister's killer and changed her mind about the sentence he is serving—life in prison without the possibility of parole. She reminds us of a core truth: that our criminal justice system cannot be just without mercy."

—Gov. George H. Ryan Sr., Governor of Illinois
1999-2003

"Every murder involves two people: the murderer and the victim. Most of us want to remain as far as we can from either one. The chasm between the two is immense, with darkness in between. But occasionally someone comes along who attempts to bridge this divide at tremendous personal risk, putting the victim's life into the killer's stare, in the hope that some light might emerge. Such a person is Jeanne Bishop, whose sister was brutally killed. She has written a mesmerizing book, *Change of Heart,* describing her difficult journey through loss to confronting evil. Reading this book takes you to places you'd rather avoid, but you may come away treasuring life even more."

—Richard C. Dieter, Executive Director,
Death Penalty Information Center

"This book is an extraordinary witness for survivors of crime and all of us who seek a more compassionate, thoughtful, and responsible way to manage the tragic ways we hurt each other. Courageous and honest, Ms. Bishop's compelling story is a gift for anyone seeking a way to think about punishment and reconciliation in a society where families are too often burdened by violence *and* the avenging politics of fear and anger."

—Bryan Stevenson, Founder and Director of the Equal Justice Initiative and author of *Just Mercy: A Story of Justice and Redemption*

"As a reporter in Arkansas covering Governor Bill Clinton in the 1980s and '90s, I watched the state murder three men, including a cop killer named Ricky Ray Rector, whose execution helped elevate Clinton to the presidency. I heard Rector moan for twenty minutes before witnessing his death. As the son of a Detroit cop, I was tangled in emotions after that experience—until I read Jeanne Bishop's extraordinary book, *Change of Heart,* and, through her painfully personal storytelling, I felt the soft power of mercy, forgiveness, and grace. Bishop's sister Nancy now lives in me, alongside the killers I watched die."

—Ron Fournier, Senior Political Columnist and Editorial Director, *National Journal*

CHANGE of HEART

CHANGE of HEART

Justice, Mercy, and Making Peace
with My Sister's Killer

JEANNE BISHOP

WESTMINSTER
JOHN KNOX PRESS
LOUISVILLE • KENTUCKY

© 2015 Jeanne Bishop

First edition
Published by Westminster John Knox Press
Louisville, Kentucky

15 16 17 18 19 20 21 22 23 24—10 9 8 7 6 5 4 3 2 1

Scripture quotations are from the New Revised Standard Version of the Bible, copyright © 1989 by the Division of Christian Education of the National Council of the Churches of Christ in the U.S.A., and are used by permission.

Book design by Erika Lundbom
Cover design by Lisa Buckley

Library of Congress Cataloging-in-Publication Data

Bishop, Jeanne.
  Change of heart : justice, mercy, and making peace with my sister's killer / Jeanne Bishop. — First edition.
    pages cm
  ISBN 978-0-664-25997-6 (alk. paper)
  1. Forgiveness—Religious aspects—Christianity. 2. Reconciliation—Religious aspects—Christianity. 3. Restorative justice—Religious aspects—Christianity. 4. Biro, David. 5. Langert, Nancy Bishop, 1964-1990. 6. Langert, Richard A., 1959-1990. 7. Murder—Illinois—Winnetka. I. Title.
  BV4647.F55B57 2015
  241'.4—dc23

                                        2014031554

PRINTED IN THE UNITED STATES OF AMERICA

♾ The paper used in this publication meets the minimum requirements of the American National Standard for Information Sciences—Permanence of Paper for Printed Library Materials, ANSI Z39.48-1992.

Westminster John Knox Press advocates the responsible use of our natural resources. The text paper of this book is made from 30 percent post-consumer waste.

Most Westminster John Knox Press books are available at special quantity discounts when purchased in bulk by corporations, organizations, and special-interest groups. For more information, please e-mail SpecialSales@wjkbooks.com.

For Nancy

CONTENTS

Part 2: What Comes After

ACKNOWLEDGMENTS

THIS STORY COULD NOT HAVE BEEN TOLD WITHOUT THE help of others. Some were part of that story; they were there. Others gave me critiques, encouragement, language, and ideas.

My two sons, Brendan and Stephen, gave me love. Their wise observations opened windows of understanding for me. When they were kicked out of the house so I could have a quiet place to write, they let me know that they understood and forgave. Their goodness and generosity overwhelm me.

People who were part of this story allowed me to tell their part of it: John Buchanan, John Boyle, Mary Pike, Randall O'Brien, Mark Osler, Hulitt Gloer, Bernardine Dohrn, Robert Gevirtz, Bud Welch, Renny Cushing,

Delbert Tibbs, Marietta Jaeger, Sister Helen Prejean, Larry Marshall, Hank Shea, Bill Pelke, Susan Stabile.

Joy Tull and Audrey Telfer dug up facts about restorative justice resources. Sara Sommervold gave helpful suggestions on my book proposal. Craig Anderson lent his keen eye and deep wisdom, challenging me to explain things in a clearer way.

David Dobson got this story from the start and helped me tell it better.

I worked on the book in some serene, beautiful places: libraries in Winnetka, Boston, and New York; an upper floor of the Fourth Presbyterian Church of Chicago; the library at Northwestern University School of Law, overlooking Lake Michigan. I'm grateful for those places and the people who opened their doors to me.

Rob Warden, champion for justice, was also a champion of this book, for which I am forever grateful.

My parents, Joyce and Lee Bishop, read to me and took me to church and sent me to good schools, including Casady School in Oklahoma City. There, my tenth-grade English teacher, the inimitable Margaret Tuck, taught me how to write.

PROLOGUE

O then come hither,
And lay my book, thy head, and heart together.

John Bunyan, *The Pilgrim's Progress*

GRAVEL CRUNCHED UNDER THE TIRES OF MY CAR AS I drove into the visitors lot at Pontiac Correctional Center on a cold Sunday morning. I rolled down my window, eyes squinting in the sunlight, to read the warning sign posted at the entrance: No weapons, no contraband, no cameras.

I pulled into a vacant spot and gathered up the few belongings I could take inside: car key, ID, two quarters to put in the locker that would store the key during my visit. I checked my coat pockets to make sure they were empty of forbidden items: cell phone, pens.

A guard in a watchtower high above a corner of the lot looked down as I opened the car door and stepped into the crisp March air. I breathed in that air, a long, deep breath. I worked in courthouses as a public defender. I was used to guards. But this felt different: I was coming not as a lawyer to see a client, but as a civilian to see a prisoner. I glanced up at the guard: Did he know who I was? Why I was there?

A long sidewalk led to the guardhouse. On my right, from a massive gray-brown stone edifice, I could hear the voices of men shouting, a melee of noise muffled by the prison's thick walls, distant and unintelligible.

I squared my shoulders, held my head up as I walked up the ramp to the guardhouse doors. Inside, two guards in dark blue uniforms, one man, one woman, sat impassively behind the counter where visitors sign in, their faces a blank. "Who are you here for?" the man asked in a bored tone.

I said the inmate's name. It felt strange on my lips, like a first cigarette or a word from another language. It was a name I had refused to speak for more than twenty years, a name I had wanted to be forgotten, consigned to a place where only God goes: the name of the person who had murdered my younger sister, her husband, and their unborn child some twenty-three years before. It was a name I'd sworn never to speak.

But God had other plans.

The guard handed me a pen, pushed a sign-in sheet across the counter, and told me to fill it out. The sheet had a series of boxes calling for information that visitors must provide: name, address, driver's license number, and so on. I was doing fine until I got to the last box: "Visitor's Relationship to Offender." I stopped, paralyzed. My pen hung in the air.

Relationship to offender? What *was* my relationship to the man whose name stung my lips? Until that moment, I would have written this: Him, murderer. Me, murder victims' family member. That was where the relationship ended. But now I would have a different one, one in which we were not categories, but human beings. I would meet him face to face. I would look into the eyes that stared down my sister in her last moments. I would hear the voice that ordered her into the basement of her comfortable suburban home, just before he put his gun to the back of her husband's head.

I would shake the hand that held that gun.

Helpless, I scanned the entries above mine searching for clues. They read, "uncle," "mother," "girlfriend," "friend."

He and I had never met, never spoken. He was not my friend.

We were not family, either. What should I call myself? Finally, I wrote the only true word I could think of: "visitor."

The guard scowled at my entry. "Are you a family member?" he asked.

"No."

"*Friend,*" he muttered, writing in the word.

I locked my car key in a small metal locker to the left of the counter, dropping into the slot the two quarters the prisoner's father had given me when he learned I was going to visit his son. He had put the two coins in my palm, then taken both my hands in his and said, "*God bless you.*"

The female guard motioned me into a small room across from the lockers and shut the door. "Take off your shoes," she told me, inspecting the inside of each one. "Turn around." She ran her hands firmly over my arms, legs, torso, in a pat-down search. "Have a nice visit," she said flatly, motioning toward the door.

The guards buzzed me through a heavy steel door that led to the building where the visit would take place. I stepped into a waiting room that had been scrubbed of personality: linoleum floor, plastic chairs, vending machines, water fountain.

I took a seat to the left of an elderly couple in windbreakers and jeans. The man was gray-haired, his face lined and creased like the folds in his jacket. He leaned forward, hands clasped between his knees, silent. The woman's hair was coiled in a tight perm around her pale face. Across the room, as if in a mirror, sat another older couple: the man's head slightly bowed, eyes on the floor, the woman staring off into the distance. From their expressions, a mixture of pain, stubborn dignity, and hope, it was clear: those couples were there to visit their sons.

No one spoke. We were waiting for the moment when names are called—not ours, but the names of the inmates we had come to see. Taut with anticipation, I fixed my eyes on the door through which the guard would come. Finally, after the parents had been called for their visits, a female guard appeared and shouted an unfamiliar name. At first I didn't respond; then I realized she had mispronounced the prisoner's name, the name I'd waited so long to speak. I jumped to my feet.

This was it. I followed into the corridor where I knew we would meet. The prisoner's father had told me the drill: guards bring the inmate out, you have an opportunity to greet one another, then you are taken to opposite sides of a thick wall of glass, a desk on either side. Those instructions gave me some comfort as I waited, heart thumping, for the prisoner to appear. At least I knew what would happen first; I had no idea what would follow.

A door at the far end of the corridor buzzed open and a tall, wiry man stepped through. He wore his brown hair short in a crew cut. The blue and white prison garb hung loosely on his frame. He looked in my direction and broke into a nervous smile. His face flushed slightly.

I walked toward him and extended my hand.

"Hello, I'm Jeanne Bishop. . . ."

Part 1

What Comes Before

Chapter 1

THE MURDERS

BELOVED READER, I HAVE A STORY TO TELL YOU. IT IS A story of change, of seeds being planted and growing, of wind blowing away debris and changing the landscape, of the impossible becoming possible.

The story is born of tragedy, of the evil, senseless taking of human lives I held most dear. My first response to that tragedy was to seal a stone over my heart, to take a rock in my hand to throw at the perpetrator, guilty as he was.

This is the story of how God rolled away that stone, loosened the fingers that gripped that rock, till it thudded in the dirt—and grew in its stead the green shoots of transformation and new life, renewal and change.

It is my story, but it is also yours, because God who loves us all and wrought this miracle in my life has the power to transform yours as well, to lead you into places you never dreamed you would go.

The story begins with a family straight out of an American fairy tale: A happy house on a tree-lined street with two parents and three girls, Jennifer, Jeanne, and Nancy. Jennifer was the oldest, I was the middle, and Nancy was the youngest. She was the bright, sunny one, the girl who loved to joke and dance and sing and tease. She was the girly one, the one who loved to cook and decorate and make crafty things. She was adored—by our parents, her sisters, her friends—because she was adorable. When Nancy was a senior at New Trier High School in Winnetka, Illinois, a school known for its theater and music programs, she landed the role of Maria in *West Side Story*. She was barely acting when she sang, "I feel charming! Oh, so charming! It's alarming how charming I feel!" She was right, after all: she was charming, and funny, and loving, and often deeply wise.

One of the people Nancy charmed was a Catholic boy from the South Side of Chicago, Richard Langert, the youngest of four boys. They had caught each other's eye when Richard was working for a company associated with my father's business. They ended up working together at the same company, Gloria Jean's Coffee Beans, Rich managing the warehouse and Nancy working in the office.

Richard courted and married her when she was young. They fit together like two pieces of a puzzle. He was a jock, a six-foot-three, 230-pound baseball and football player, the Gentle Giant, as he was nicknamed. She was the music and theater geek whose skin was as soft and pale as his was hard and tanned. He was strong and silent; she was the comedienne. He basked in the radiant glow she cast; she leaned on him for support. They reveled in each other's company. Richard often had to work weekend nights at the warehouse, so Nancy made sure that Sunday mornings were always sacred—their time together. If you walked by their bedroom on a Sunday morning, as I happened to do one day when they were staying at my parents' home, you would hear the sound of their laughter floating through the door. Laughter was a familiar sound around them.

On the Friday nights when Richard was away at work, I would take the train from downtown Chicago to Nancy and Richard's cozy apartment on Tower Road in Winnetka, a few blocks from the Hubbard Woods train stop. Nancy and I would put on sweats and climb under a blanket on their couch, our backs resting on either end and our feet meeting in the middle, sharing a bowl of popcorn and a Hitchcock movie.

Their set point was happy. Their tastes were simple. I got to travel with them once, on a trip to Scotland not long before they were killed. The theaters and sights and restaurants of Edinburgh were fun, but what Nancy and Richard truly loved was small and quiet: the tiny northern town of Pitlochry. The stone walls and rosebushes, the churches nestled in the hills—a bit of Nancy's and Richard's hearts stayed there when we left. When we returned home, she showed me a photo she had taken of the town: "This is what heaven will look like," she said.

Nancy had no lofty career goals; what she wanted more than anything was to be a wife and a mom. She wanted a house with a white picket fence, literally. After their wedding, Nancy and Richard set out right away to have a baby.

She devoted herself to the project: she shunned junk food, avoided cigarette smoke, took vitamins, wished and prayed. When Nancy found out she was pregnant, she was over the moon. She rushed out to buy baby bottles, arranging them in a neat row on a kitchen shelf. She was twenty-five years old.

To celebrate the pregnancy, I gathered with Nancy, Richard, and my mother and father on the night before Palm Sunday in 1990 at a cozy Italian restaurant on Chicago's North Side. It was the perfect place—warm and fragrant; a big table set with candlelight; pasta, wine, and laughter. Nancy joked happily about gaining baby weight. My parents beamed contentedly; the grandchild they had longed for was at last to come. I gave Nancy a baby gift, a soft, hand-knitted baby sweater I had picked up on a recent trip. As we hugged our good-byes in the parking lot in back of the restaurant, I talked with Nancy about coming over the next day, after church. "See you tomorrow," I said as we parted. It is a phrase I have never spoken since: those words now seem to me a tempter of fate, a foretelling of doom. I had no idea as I said them to her, hugging her warm body and smelling the perfume she loved to wear, that it was her last night on earth.

After we left the restaurant, I returned alone to my apartment near the Chicago lakefront. My parents went back to their large suburban home. Nancy and

Richard drove back to the townhouse they were staying in, owned by my parents, in one of the safest and most affluent communities in America, the North Shore enclave of Winnetka.

At that same moment, an intruder was using a glass cutter to break through the sliding glass back door of Nancy and Richard's home. Dressed in black and wearing gloves, he silently stacked the pieces of glass he had shorn away on the ground; he knew that smashing the glass would alert the neighbors, who might call the police. He entered the townhouse and looked around. He positioned a chair in the middle of the living room so that he could see every entrance to the townhouse: the front door, the side door, the back.

Then he sat down and waited.

When Nancy and Richard returned to the townhouse, their killer had a loaded gun in his hand: a .357 Magnum revolver he had stolen just two days earlier. Richard immediately began bargaining for their lives. He told the intruder that Nancy was pregnant. Richard offered whatever they had in the townhouse: jewelry, electronics, $500 in cash Nancy had gotten when she'd cashed a paycheck at the bank earlier that day. Police evidence technicians later found the money strewn on the ground, as if it had been tossed there.

Nancy and Richard's dog, a cocker spaniel named Pepsi, suddenly ran into the room and startled the intruder; nervously, he squeezed the trigger of the gun and fired a bullet into the living room wall. "All right," Richard told the gunman, "someone is going to hear that and call the police. Why don't you lock us in the basement and leave?" The killer appeared to assent.

Gun still pointed at them, he handcuffed Richard and ordered the couple into the basement.

But he didn't lock them in and go; instead, he put the gun to the back of Richard's head and fired once, killing him instantly. Nancy watched in horror as her husband slumped to the floor. Then the killer turned the gun on her. She huddled in a corner, protecting her head with her arms. He fired two shots into her side and abdomen, the bullets ripping into her pregnant belly. Then he fled, leaving Nancy to die along with her husband and the child she was carrying.

A coroner estimated that Nancy lived for about fifteen minutes after that. Marks on her body and the evidence at the crime scene tell the story of what she did in her last moments.

Bruises and scrapes on her elbows and a trail of her blood marked her course: she dragged herself to a basement shelf and banged on it with a heavy tool, in a desperate call for help. The shelf was riddled with indentations. At some point, she must have realized that no help would come, that she was dying. Nancy dragged herself by her elbows again, to where her husband lay dead. Next to his body she wrote a message of love in her own blood: the shape of a heart and the letter *u*.

Love you.

It was the way she had signed letters to Richard over the years. She died there next to him.

The next day was Palm Sunday. I was suited up in my choir robe, unaware of what had happened the night before, holding a palm branch and a folder full of music in the back of Fourth Presbyterian Church of Chicago. I loved the church; it reminded me of the Presbyterian churches I had grown up in: big congregation, intellectually challenging preaching, glorious music. I was about to walk up the center aisle for the opening hymn. Just as I was about to go in, I felt a gentle hand on my arm. Startled, I turned to see the church secretary. "You have a phone call," she said.

"Sorry?" I replied. It made no sense; who would be calling me at church? "Um, could you take a message?" "No," she replied firmly. "You need to come with me." My heart started to pound. This was something serious. My mind raced: could it be my father? A heart attack, maybe?

The secretary led me to her office, where the receiver of her telephone was off the hook and sitting on her desk, waiting for me. I stood in front of the desk and reached for the phone.

"You need to sit down," the secretary said.

"I'm OK, really," I answered.

"*Sit down,*" she told me. I obeyed.

My heart pounding, I pulled the receiver to my ear and managed a tentative "Hello?" My father replied, "Jeanne?" I breathed out with relief. It wasn't him.

But then my next thought was, if it wasn't him, who was it? My mom?

I wasn't prepared for the words my father spoke next: "Nancy and Richard have been killed."

Those words hung in the air as I tried to absorb them. *Nancy and Richard have been killed.*

"What?" I exclaimed. My body froze. "What do you mean, they have been killed?" It seemed impossible.

They were young, in their twenties, full of life. How could they be dead? An image flashed into my mind: Nancy and Richard in their small car, swerving on the highway to avoid a semitrailer truck bearing down on them, smashing into an embankment.

"Someone killed them," my father said.

My reeling mind tried to collect and process what he was saying: *found in their basement . . . blood everywhere. . . .* Nancy and Richard were so good, so innocent. They had so much to live for. The thought that anyone would deliberately take their lives was inconceivable to me. How could anyone look into Nancy's shining eyes and mercilessly snuff out the light in them?

My dad told me to stay there at the church; Dr. Gilbert Bowen, the pastor of his church in Kenilworth, where Nancy and Richard were married, was coming to pick me up. He would take me to meet my family where they were gathered at the Winnetka police station.

I hung up the phone, stunned. Then I leaned back on the couch in the church office and started to cry. The secretary silently handed me tissues. We didn't speak; I couldn't. For the next forty-five minutes as I sat there and sobbed, waiting for Dr. Bowen to get me, my heart raged: *Why? Why, God? Why them? She was only twenty-five years old.* By the time he arrived, I had built up a steam of anger and indignation at God for allowing this senseless slaughter. I got into Dr. Bowen's car and let loose a barrage of insistent questions. Where was Nancy now? I knew where her body was, lying in the townhouse, a crime scene roped off with yellow police tape. But where was *she,* her spirit? She must have been praying when she encountered her killer; why hadn't God heard her prayers to be spared, for her husband and baby to be spared? How could God let her life end before she had gotten to fulfill her dream of being a mom?

I don't remember what Dr. Bowen said in response. It could have been the wisest counsel in the world; I wouldn't have heard it. I remember only this: him waiting in the car outside my apartment on Chestnut Street, a few blocks from the church. We stopped there so I could get some belongings—toothbrush, pajamas, clothes—since I knew I'd need to stay with my family at my parents' home in Winnetka. I blindly parted some hangers in my closet and pulled out a dress. As soon as I took it in my hand, I burst into tears again. I was holding a black dress. *I am picking out a dress for my sister's funeral*, I thought.

Dr. Bowen took me to the police station, where I found my parents waiting. They were ashen-faced. My mother's eyes were wide with shock. She spoke slowly, in a voice that sounded as if it were coming from a distant cave; she moved as if she were under water.

The police came in and told us the cause of Nancy and Richard's death, which hadn't been certain until that moment: they had been shot. I pictured someone breaking into their home, maybe two men, pointing a gun in the dark and firing. I tried to fathom it, tried to understand what would cause someone to do such a horrible thing. As I did, I spoke for the first time since arriving at the station. It wasn't a thought I had formulated; it just emerged. I heard myself saying these words to the assembled group: "I don't want to hate anyone."

It startled even me: *I don't want to hate anyone.* I think I grasped at that moment that evil had intruded into our lives. I could not ignore it. It was too vast and terrible not to change me. It required a response. I knew, even then, that I could not allow that response to be hatred. That would take me away from who Nancy was, someone who loved, and move me closer to who the killer was, someone who could snuff out the life of another human being with the squeeze of a trigger. Whoever he was, I would not hate him.

The act was evil: how could he have looked into her bright eyes, heard her sweet voice, and fired the bullets that would put out that light, still that voice forever? And yet, I knew that if I regarded the person who committed that act as evil, if I let that person turn me to bitterness toward him, I would drift unmoored into an endless ocean of hate. Nancy was about love and life. She was carrying life within her body when she died. She would never have wanted hatred and vengeance to be her memorial. I clung to the thought of *her*, not the one who had killed her.

We left the police station and were allowed to go see Nancy's body at the townhouse. We were not allowed to see Richard—maybe because of the ghastly damage done by the bullet to his head. I identified his body later at the county morgue, not in person but via a photo. His face was almost unrecognizable. The morgue gave me some of Nancy's and Richard's belongings before I left, including the glasses Richard was wearing the night he was killed. They were covered in blood.

When we got to the townhouse, Nancy was lying on a gurney inside a dark plastic body bag. A police officer unzipped the top of the bag so we could see her face. It was frozen in death. Her eyes were open, looking upward; her lips were parted slightly. I could see dried blood in her mouth. I touched her body through the bag. It was not the soft, warm body I had hugged close the night before; it was hard, immobile. My heart fell like a stone in water. Nevermore. Nevermore to see the light on her hair or smell her perfumed sweaters or touch her warm skin. Nevermore to hear her footsteps as she walked through a door. She was gone.

I had no thought of God in that moment; there was no God here, only emptiness, the terrifying void of death where life once was. I stared at Nancy's body, numb with disbelief. You could have sliced my flesh open with a knife; I would not have flinched, or even felt it.

We walked out of the townhouse into a night lit by the blinding glare of the media. News trucks encircled the house. Our every movement was being recorded as we left the place where Nancy and Richard took their last breaths. We were on the nightly news that night, and for many nights to come.

The next few days were a fog of grief. I didn't sleep that first night: when I closed the door to the guest bedroom in my parents' house, the darkness was too dark. *It is like a tomb,* I thought. *Like being buried in a grave.* I got up in the morning, looked in the bathroom mirror, and picked up a toothbrush, only to stop and hold it in midair. *Why should I brush my teeth?* I thought. *Put on makeup, get dressed? I can never be happy again. I will never smile again.*

In those first few hours I remember being less angry at whoever had killed Nancy than I was at God. I understood that people have free will to choose evil, that there are those among us who make that choice. I knew Nancy was a Christian; she would have been praying from the moment she walked in her home and saw a gun pointed at her. *God, help me,* she must have begged. *Save me. Save my husband; save our baby.* How could God have ignored that prayer, have let her die? It made a mockery of psalms like the ones I had grown up with, about how God is an ever-present help in trouble (Ps. 46:1), a refuge and fortress (Ps. 91). That seemed a cruel lie.

A steady stream of people came to our house, bearing casseroles and cakes and giving us long, silent hugs. A small group of my mother's friends dubbed themselves The Shiva Squad, named after the Jewish tradition of sitting shiva, a weeklong mourning period. Some Jewish, some Christian, some none of the above, the women took over, answering the doorbell, making pots of tea, putting stuff away. They didn't ask; they just came and stayed. I would walk into the kitchen at any time of day and see one of them wiping the counters and another answering the phone. One would be running around vacuuming crumbs from the carpet; another would be making a big pot of split pea soup. I will love them as long as I live.

One set of visitors wasn't so welcome, though, to my father especially: the press. When the first reporters came to our door, he was beside himself. I gently asked him if I could speak to them. I had been a journalism major at Northwestern's Medill School of Journalism and had worked for newspapers, and I knew this for a fact: not one of those reporters wanted to draw that assignment, to be the one to ask the grieving family, "How do you feel?" I stepped outside to talk with them on the front steps and shut the door.

"I know you don't want to be here," I told them, bowing my head. They nodded vigorously. "I know your editor sent you. Tell me what you need." They needed a photo of Nancy and Richard; I got them one. I promised we would release a statement later. We did, one I wrote on behalf of our family, calling Nancy and Richard "the light of our lives," thanking people for their sympathy and prayers, and affirming that Nancy, Richard, and their baby were safe in the arms of God.

I believed that. But still I struggled. How could a loving God have stood by while Nancy bled to death on a cold basement floor?

That question tore at my heart as I sat in a pew beside my mother in Kenilworth Union Church. It was the day of Nancy and Richard's funeral, at the church where they had been married not long before. The same pastor who presided over their wedding was now conducting their memorial service. I read out loud for the congregation the same chapter I'd read at their wedding: 1 Corinthians 13. The final words of the chapter seemed to reveal their meaning to me in a completely new way, even as I spoke them: *When I was a child, I spoke like a child, I thought like a child, I reasoned like a child; when I became an adult, I put an end to childish ways. For now we see in a mirror, dimly, but then we will see face to face. Now I know only in part; then I will know fully, even as I have been fully known. And now faith, hope, and love abide, these three; and the greatest of these is love.*

I was that child, the child who wanted to know *now*. I knew I would have to wait until I saw God face to face to have the answer I longed for to my question: *why?*

I struggled with something else, too, a horror movie that played in my head on a continuous loop: Saturday night, April 7, 1990. Nancy and Richard walk through the front door of their townhouse, chatting happily after the night out to dinner. Nancy is still carrying the present for the baby. In the murky shadows before they turn on the light, they see a shape. Someone is pointing a gun at them. He orders them to lie face down on the floor. They beg for their lives. Unrelenting, he takes them into the basement. Nancy hears the shot go off, sees her husband slump to the floor. The barrel of the gun turns toward her. . . .

The darkness of it overwhelmed me. I stopped eating and sleeping. I lost ten pounds in one week from an already thin frame. I turned for help to the pastor of my church, the Rev. John Buchanan. I met him in his office at the church on a dark April afternoon and told him about that horror movie, my nightmare of Nancy's last moments.

John listened carefully, then turned his hands palms up and balled them into fists. "You are holding on like *this*," he said, fists clutched in front of him. "It is too much for you. You cannot bear up under it. You have to open your hands and hold it up, like *this*," he added, unclenching his hands and raising his two open palms toward heaven. "Hold it up to God and say, 'This is too much for me. God, take it and redeem it.'"

The simple truth of it stunned me. He was right. I was gripping the tragedy tight to my breast, when all along, God was there, able to take the broken pieces and transform them. I walked out of John's office breathing a prayer: *Take this from me, God. Do something with it. Bring good out of this evil.*

Little did I know then how powerfully God would answer that prayer.

Nor did I know then how the path of my own life would change. Not every moment is equal; some moments are the fulcrum upon which our lives turn. That Palm Sunday was an unequal moment, one that pushed me into darkness. I did not know then whether that darkness was a cave or a tunnel; nor did I foresee the wondrous ways God would lead me out.

Chapter 2

THE ARREST

IN THE WEEKS AFTER NANCY'S DEATH, I STOPPED QUESTION-
ing God and started questioning myself. If I got to live
longer than Nancy, what would I do to honor her memory, to live a life worthy of hers? Her life had ended at
age twenty-five. I'd already had four years longer on
this earth. I knew I couldn't waste one more minute of
the days I had been given.

And wasting it I was. I had started law school years
before with the intention of making the world a better
place. What law school taught me was important was
this: Make the best grades. Be hired by a large, prestigious law firm. Earn a big salary. That became my idea
of success, and I achieved it. At the time Nancy died,
I was working in downtown Chicago at Mayer Brown,

a global firm that paid me well as an associate doing corporate work.

Two problems plagued me in that work, however. The first was one I should have thought about before I took the job: I was being paid a lot because I had to work a lot. Billable hours ruled. I worked nights, weekends, holidays. I missed gatherings with friends, family. I was constantly apologizing, telling people how sorry I was I couldn't come. I remember one gorgeous weekend day, standing at my office window, my nose pressed to the glass, looking out at the happy people on the streets below. I longed to be them.

The second problem with corporate work was that I was terrible at it. I didn't care much about the work; it seemed empty and meaningless to me, pieces of paper bearing numbers with a lot of zeros at the end. The firm that had hired me in good faith and was paying my salary was rewarded with a halfhearted effort. I knew that was wrong, that the firm's partners and clients deserved better. Colossians 3:23 convicted me: "Whatever your task, put yourselves into it, as done for the Lord and not for your masters." I was failing miserably at that. The law firm was not getting the best of me. That, I gave to the pro bono work I did.

I loved that work: representing refugees seeking asylum in America, helping artists and activists set up not-for-profit corporations, doing human rights work in Northern Ireland. I was good at it because it mattered to me.

When Nancy died at age twenty-five, it was as if a bucket of icy water had been tossed in my face. It was the starkest wake-up call imaginable. Nancy's murder taught me this: Life is short. It can be taken at any second. None of us have a moment to waste. Pride and fear were why I had taken the corporate law position—pride in the status of a job with a big firm, and fear of not having enough money if I worked at a place that paid less. The gift of life I had been given was too precious to squander on something as small as fear or as misguided as pride. I wanted to do something meaningful to honor Nancy and the Giver of that gift.

I told the firm I planned to leave. The lawyers of Mayer Brown were as gracious to me in my departure as they were when they hired me. The firm gave me a month off with pay in the aftermath of the murders. One of the partners, Howard "Scott" McCue, knew I was the administrator of Nancy and Richard's estate; without being asked, he quietly announced that he would wind up that estate for me. I thanked him profusely and asked how I would be billed for the work; he refused any payment.

The firm's help was a godsend: I could barely read Nancy and Richard's will without grief twisting my heart. Nancy had specified what she wanted done with her most precious possessions: an antique secretary; a Boehm porcelain bird; her beloved cocker spaniel, Pepsi. The love that went into those things!

The job I wanted was with the Law Office of the Cook County Public Defender in Chicago, which defends people in criminal cases who cannot afford to hire a private attorney to represent them. Some friends were puzzled by my choice: after the murders of my loved ones, why become a defense lawyer and not a prosecutor? The reason was simple: I knew what it was like to need a lawyer myself.

Around the time Nancy and Richard were murdered, I had been going to Northern Ireland to do human rights work. This was during the Troubles, the conflict in Northern Ireland between those who wanted the country to remain in the United Kingdom and those who were seeking a united Ireland. I was a legal observer in so-called Diplock courts, in which there was no right to a jury trial. I interviewed people who had been detained under laws that allowed the security forces to hold people in custody for up to seven days without charge or right to counsel. I wrote reports about killings of unarmed civilians by the police and British army, torture by the security forces, the reversal of a suspect's right to silence.

The FBI took note. I was meeting with people who were considered threats by one of the United States' closest allies, Great Britain. When Nancy and Richard were found dead, it gave FBI agents the perfect opportunity to use the murder investigation to investigate me and the people I knew in Ireland. They seized that opportunity.

One night within a week of the murders, I was at my parents' house, exhausted and needing respite. I was curled up on the big brown couch in the cozy loft of the house, pulling books off the shelf. I found a Bible that bore an inscription stating that the book had been given to Nancy by her church when she was ten years old and in fourth grade. She had written on the inside cover, in her childlike hand, "I love Mommy. I love Daddy. I love Jenny. I love Jeanne." My heart constricted in pain. That was Nancy; it was exactly what she would do—record in the precious book she prized the names of those she loved most, treasures within a treasure.

I carefully put Nancy's Bible back on the shelf. Just then, the phone rang. I ran downstairs to answer it. It was the Winnetka Police. The FBI wanted to talk to me, they said, about Northern Ireland. They thought there could be a connection to the murders. The FBI's theory was this: someone in Ireland believed that my human rights work there was a cover for what was mistakenly believed to be my true mission, to spy for the U.S. government. According to this theory, the Irish Republican Army (IRA) then set out to kill me and mistook Nancy for me. The police officer on the other end of the phone explained that the FBI wanted to talk to me about the people I knew in Ireland. Would I come in to the police station and meet with them, as soon as possible?

I arranged a time and hung up the phone in disbelief. I sat there at the kitchen desk, paralyzed. How could this be? The theory was preposterous. The IRA did not target Americans. It always claimed responsibility for its acts, even its mistakes. Nancy and I looked nothing alike; it would have been hard to confuse us. I was easy to find; my home address and telephone number were in the phone book. Then it hit me: the FBI didn't want to know the names of people I knew because it wanted to solve the murders; it wanted to use the murder investigation to get the names. From that standpoint, the longer the investigation stayed open, the longer the murders went unsolved, the better.

A wave of horror rose up in me. I had a vision of a man sitting in a bar somewhere in Chicago watching a news brief that the FBI was looking for the suspect in the Langert murders in *Ireland*. That man was laughing. Laughing, thinking, *I'm going to get away with this.* Knowing the trail to him was growing cold.

I picked up the phone again and called someone who knew about the FBI and the IRA, the civil rights lawyer Mary Pike. Mary and her law partner Stephen Somerstein had for years represented a former IRA man, Joseph Doherty, who had escaped from custody in Northern Ireland and come to New York. He lived and worked in the area for sixteen months until one morning FBI agents arrested him at his job. Mary and Steve successfully fought off the U.S. government's attempt to send Doherty back to Northern Ireland for about a decade. I should have known Mary was working, even late at night; her assistant, Lynn, told me I could find her in an alcove of the bar association library near Mary's office. I prayed I would reach her.

I did, to my relief. I told her about the request I'd just gotten from the Winnetka Police, the meeting I'd arranged with the FBI. I laid out their theory, told her how panicked I was at the thought of Nancy and Richard's murder investigation being hijacked. She listened, said how sorry she was that I was going through this, asked a few questions. "Mary," I pleaded, "what should I do?"

She responded in the sober, level tone she uses when laying out important facts, "You have a choice. You can give information about innocent people in Ireland,

and they will be hurt; or, you can refuse to give that information, and you will be hurt."

I loved her for it. She had framed it perfectly; that was the choice, exactly—not a difficult choice at all, when put that way. I drew a deep breath and thanked her. My course was clear.

I went into that meeting with the police and FBI and told them this: I will tell you anything you want to know about me. I will tell you nothing about innocent people I know in Ireland. I think your theory is ridiculous. I will not help you steer this investigation toward Belfast and away from Winnetka. Do the good, solid police work that will find the real killer.

That choice began a six-month investigation of me which ended only when Nancy's killer was arrested. My apartment was searched. My phone calls were monitored. People who phoned me got a visit or a call from the FBI. FBI agents came to Mayer Brown and flashed their badges, announcing that they needed to speak to me. The U.S. Department of Justice convened a grand jury about me and subpoenaed a close friend to testify. The story was leaked to the press, and I became a headline: *Victim's sister uncooperative in murder investigation.*

I was not yet a criminal defense lawyer, but I knew I needed one. I had the means to hire an attorney; all I had to do was write a check. But what about the people who did not have the resources I had? I wondered. When they were in the crosshairs of the government, with all its power, they needed a lawyer, too—a good one. I wanted to be that lawyer.

I applied to the public defender's office. During my interview, the head of the office at the time, Randolph

Stone, was skeptical. He contrasted the salary I was leaving at Mayer Brown with the one he could afford to offer me. I would be making a third of what I had earned before. "How are you going to live?" he asked. I told him: I had paid off my debts (student loans, car) and had saved up the equivalent of a year's salary. I lived in a rented studio apartment with no kitchen, not a luxurious condo with a hefty mortgage. I was ready.

Stone believed me, apparently, and hired me. I was due to start working as a public defender in November 1990, just months after Nancy and Richard had been killed. I was eager to begin a new chapter in my life. I did not see what was coming.

One cold October night, on the eve of starting the new job, I got a telephone call at my apartment downtown. "Jay Levine, Channel 2 News," rasped the voice on the other end of the line. "I'm calling to get your reaction to the arrest in your sister's murder case."

Dumbfounded, I asked, "Arrest? What arrest?"

Levine told me that a teenager had been picked up for the crime and was in custody at the Winnetka police station.

His name was David Biro.

David Biro. At last, I had a name, an identity, for the faceless person who killed Nancy.

"I have to go," I told him, and hung up. I called the Winnetka Police immediately.

Police confirmed what the reporter had told me: they were holding a local teen. He was a student in his junior year at New Trier, the well-regarded public high school in Winnetka, the same school Nancy had attended. He was under arrest for the murders and was being questioned by prosecutors. Heart racing, I jumped in my car and headed to my parents' home in Winnetka, wanting to be there when any news broke.

When I arrived, the place was buzzing with people, waiting, wondering. When the phone rang, I answered it. The man on the other end of the line was David Biro's father, Nick Biro.

I was stunned. I knew Mr. Biro; he had worked with my father years before in another city altogether: Oklahoma City, Oklahoma. They were both executives at Wilson Foods, which was headquartered there. Nick and his wife, Joan Biro, and my parents knew one another, but we girls—my sisters and I—had never met the Biro children. I remembered, though, seeing the Biro family's holiday cards to our family over the years, always a group photo of the Biro parents with their three children, a girl and two boys. *I have seen an image of Nancy's killer: a little boy on a Christmas card*, it struck me. It felt surreal.

Now Nick was calling about that boy, his youngest child, David. Nick's voice was ragged; it sounded as if he had swallowed broken glass. I don't remember his exact words, something about being terribly sorry for our family tragedy, but that it couldn't possibly have been his son who committed the crime. There had to be some mistake.

I don't recall exactly what I said, either, something to the effect that we would be in litigation soon and not able to talk. I do remember what I didn't say, though: how sorry I was for him, how terrible I felt for him that his child was under arrest for murder. The weight of that must have been crushing.

In the weeks that followed, my family learned facts about David Biro that turned our stomachs. He had bragged about killing Nancy and Richard to the high school friend who turned David in. David had a long history of violence, including shooting at passersby out of the window of his home with a BB gun and once attempting to poison his family by tainting their milk with rat poison. After that last incident, he was sent temporarily to a mental health facility called Charter Barclay. David left the institution on a weekend pass and told his parents he didn't like it there; they didn't make him go back.

Police learned through this classmate that David had confessed to stealing computer equipment from New Trier High School. With that information, police got a warrant to search his home, just a few blocks from where Nancy and Richard lived, and found the equipment, with "NT" stenciled prominently in blue on the side, in David's third-floor bedroom.

Police found more in that bedroom: the .357 Magnum revolver David had used to kill my family members. It was a gun he'd stolen from the office of a local attorney, the same attorney his mother had hired to defend David after he'd forged an application to buy a gun. Also found were speed loaders and .38-caliber bullets like the ones found in my sister's body. Handcuffs of the brand on Richard's wrists when his body was found. Burglary tools. The glass cutter David had used to break in. Perhaps most chilling of all, a trophy notebook he had kept with press clippings about the murders and a poem he had written about it. "I am Cain," the poem read, a reference to the biblical character who kills his brother. "I kill people." We learned from police that David had even attended Nancy and Richard's funeral.

David's family hired another attorney to defend him in the murder case, the best there was: Robert Gevirtz. Gevirtz was, ironically, a former Cook County assistant public defender. He had risen to the highest ranks of the office before he left to start a private practice. He had a well-earned reputation for integrity, diligence, and civility.

I wasn't expecting to meet Gevirtz before the murder trial, but I did. Just after I started my job as a public defender in November 1990, my new workplace held a party at a downtown hotel to commemorate the sixtieth anniversary of the Office of the Cook County Public Defender. I went to the party, anticipating little more than cocktails and speeches. Instead, a friend and fellow lawyer, Deborah Gubin, approached me with a startling request.

"Bob Gevirtz is here," she said in a low voice, looking at me intently. "He noticed that you were, too, and didn't want to alarm or upset you. He wanted you to know that he would like to meet you if you are willing."

I was struck by his consideration. The lawyer for my sister's killer didn't approach me unannounced, blindside me; he sent an emissary, someone I knew as a trusted friend, to see if he would be welcome. "Of course I will meet him," I answered. Debbie went off to find him.

She returned a few minutes later, bringing in tow a tall, thin, bespectacled man with dark curly hair and a gentle expression. She left us alone. "I'm Bob Gevirtz," he said as he took my hand. "I want you to know that what I'm about to do has nothing to do with how terrible I feel about what has happened to your family."

It was a moment of grace. It was a lesson for me, as a lawyer, I have never forgotten. Be kind. Be honest. Acknowledge the suffering of victims and their survivors. Say words of consolation. Gevirtz and I became friends, and remain so. If someone I loved were ever in trouble, he is the person I would call.

I was grateful for Gevirtz from the beginning; I knew I could trust him to do a good job in the most important trial of my life, the trial of my sister's killer. It was to come soon, and would set me on a path I never anticipated, toward advocating for mercy for the very people who had committed crimes like David Biro's, and, one day, for David himself.

This grace, too, came at a time when I had been shattered. The murders were enough to do that, of course, but the investigation targeting me compounded the hurt. I was covered in broken places, but it is into those broken places that grace can seep, the strongest of healing waters.

Chapter 3

THE TRIAL

Many families of murder victims have to wait years for their loved one's case to go to trial, each one of these days dragging on in the long, upward slog toward justice. In that respect, my family and I were lucky; we didn't have to wait long for trial. That had to do with David Biro himself.

It can take years for murder cases to go to trial in Cook County, Illinois, for a variety of reasons: long pretrial investigations, crowded court dockets, the desire of some defense lawyers to "age" a case in the hopes that passions will subside or witnesses disappear. David Biro's case was scheduled to go to trial in only a year.

Biro wanted it that way. He was being held without bond in the Cook County Jail, a bleak and violent place. Situated on Chicago's southwest side, the jail houses approximately 10,000 inmates at a time. The inmates wear khaki scrubs and laceless shoes. Prisoners get fresh air and exercise for only a small portion of the day. They live on a diet of bologna sandwiches wrapped in plastic. Gangs are rampant. Violent assaults are common. The noise is relentless. The jail is as different from the safe, quiet streets and million-dollar homes in the suburb where David Biro grew up as the moon is from the earth. I imagined that he did not want to stay there a moment longer than he had to.

Nor did Biro intend to assert an insanity defense, that he was not guilty of the murders because he was not sane when he committed them. He could have attempted to mount such a defense, especially in light of his brief stint at the psychiatric hospital, Charter Barclay. But Biro surely would have been advised by his lawyer, one of the most competent in Chicago, that a successful insanity defense would not result in Biro's freedom; rather, it would likely result in a lifetime of psychiatric treatment in a locked facility. To get out, Biro would have to rely, instead, on the defense that the state would not be able to prove him guilty beyond a reasonable doubt.

The trial was to take place at the Cook County Criminal Courts Building in Chicago, known as 26th and California, for the intersection of the grimy, wind-swept streets where it sits. The building is a massive gray structure next to the jail with slow, creaky elevators and a lingering cockroach problem.

The trial judge was Shelvin Singer, a well-regarded, seasoned jurist known for his bookish nature and scrupulous thoroughness.

The trial team for the defense was Gevirtz and his law partner, Dennis Born, a blond, balding man in his forties. The team for the prosecution, the Office of the Cook County State's Attorney, consisted of a deep bench of career assistant state's attorneys who had the experience to mount a case as high profile as this one. They were led by Pat O'Brien, a dogged prosecutor—now a judge—who had achieved a slew of convictions on murder cases.

Nancy and Richard's murder trial was a big press case. While shootings were common on Chicago's South and West sides, the wealthy North Shore Village of Winnetka hadn't seen an unsolved murder for about a century. Before Nancy's, there had been only one murder in the past hundred years: in 1988, a deranged woman named Laurie Dann burst into a Winnetka elementary school and shot six children, killing one, eight-year-old Nicholas Corwin. She then took her own life. (After Nancy and Richard and their unborn baby were found shot to death, my mother and father received a beautiful gold box with three white flowers in it. Nicky Corwin's parents had sent it.)

The press had been calling our family since the murders happened, seeking interviews, but we never gave them. Police and prosecutors told us that anything we said to reporters might jeopardize the criminal case against David Biro, and we believed them. Except for our initial written statement just after the murders were discovered, we said nothing at all publicly. We wanted to wait to speak until the case was over.

My family members were due to speak at the trial, though; my parents and older sister were to be witnesses. My mother was to be the "life and death" witness, the one who testifies that the murder victim, on a particular day when last seen, was in fact a person who was once alive. My father would be called to testify about the agonizing moment when he walked into the townhouse where Nancy and Richard lived and discovered their bodies frozen in death.

Because witnesses are excluded from viewing the testimony of other witnesses, my family members could not sit through the whole trial. But I could. I vowed not to miss a minute of it.

∞

On November 4, 1991, I woke early with a jolt: *today is the day.*

I took a quick shower and dressed in black, my way of remembering Nancy on that day. I met my parents, and we went to the courthouse together, tense with anticipation. I stayed with my father as we ran the gauntlet of television cameras following us as we went in. He was walking slowly, debilitated by the cancer he had been suffering since before Biro's arrest. I didn't want the press to pick him off to ask him questions, the way a lion picks off the slowest antelope in the herd.

We stepped onto the crowded, antiquated elevator to ride to the fifth floor where our courtroom was.

Lawyers holding stacks of files, members of the public looking anxious, police officers in uniform coming to testify in court—we all huddled against one another as the elevator shuddered upward. No one spoke.

The courtroom, Room 504, was a stately, high-ceilinged room. It smelled of wood and dust and old books. The grayish light from outside filtered in through tall windows on the right. The well of the court, where the court personnel were stationed—judge, lawyers, clerk, sheriff, court reporter—was separated by a waist-high wall. The area for the public on the other side of that wall was lined with hard, wooden benches. I slid onto one near the front and started looking around, noticing things: the courtroom sketch artist with his pad and colored pencils, the stacks of exhibits and photographs near the counsel tables, the door to the sheriff's lockup. That was the door David Biro would soon walk through, I knew, and I fixed my eyes on that spot. It would be my first sight of him in person.

When the sheriffs brought him into the courtroom, gasps erupted from some of the spectators gathered with me on the benches. I almost gasped myself. The tall, lanky young man with a shock of brown hair walked in with his head erect, his eyes flashing cool confidence as he looked at us. His gait was unhurried, a shambling walk; his expression was almost a sneer. *I am the Master of the Universe*, it seemed to say. *I am not afraid of you.*

As he sat down between his lawyers at the defense counsel table, he looked out with piercing eyes that seemed not to blink. When he looked at me, I stared back. *I am not going to look away first,* I thought. *I am not afraid of you, either.* We locked eyes for what seemed like ages till at last he turned his away.

I could feel anger rising up in me, not a burning rage, but a steely, cold determination to see him brought down. I remembered my first thought, from the police station, when I learned Nancy had been murdered: *I don't want to hate anyone.* Could I keep that promise to myself?

Next to enter the courtroom were the jurors, brought by one of the sheriffs from a conference room behind the judge's bench. They shuffled in, a modestly dressed assortment of men and women, looking sober and carrying notepads and pencils. As they took their seats in the jury box, I looked at each one intently, with eyes that silently begged them, *See me. I am Nancy's family. We are here.*

The prosecution's opening statement was workmanlike and thorough, laying out in stark detail the evidence O'Brien and his team would present. Murders, crime scene, evidence technicians, confession, search warrant, gun, handcuffs, glass cutter, notebook, bloody clothes, bullets, ballistics tests. The jurors were still and attentive, some quietly taking notes.

The prosecution put on a series of witnesses: my mom, police, the coroner, the classmate who had turned in Biro, a young man whom David had told of killing my family members—and of how he was planning to kill again, the next intended victim a security guard at a bank in Winnetka. The classmate described in detail David's confession to murdering my loved ones and testified that David told him, "They deserved to die anyhow. They were annoying." My heart twisted at this description of Nancy and Richard. *No. They didn't deserve to die. They had everything to live for.*

Then came the defense case. The star witness was David Biro himself. I was shocked when he took the stand; defense lawyers rarely want to put their clients on, for fear they will be taken apart during the wide-ranging questions prosecutors are allowed to ask on cross-examination. As soon as David started talking and his story began taking shape, though, I could see his purpose. He wasn't claiming insanity or some impulsive, less culpable reason for killing my family members; he was blaming the crime on someone else. *He wants to get away scot-free*, I thought. *This is the only way.*

David's story was simple but ingenious: He said that yes, he had taken the gun from his lawyer's office and, yes, that gun was the one that had killed Nancy and Richard. But, David said, he hadn't gone to Nancy and Richard's home or fired that gun. Someone else did. That someone else, he said, was a friend of his, another Winnetka teen with a history of brushes with the law. Biro told jurors that after he had stolen the .357 Magnum revolver from his lawyer's office, he gave it to this friend to sell. Instead, David claimed, the friend kept the gun and used it to kill Nancy and Richard. He then came to David's house at eleven o'clock on the night of the murders, ringing the doorbell and asking David to keep the gun for him. "I just shot two people with it," Biro claimed this friend told him.

The story was absurd—if this friend had wanted to get rid of a gun that could tie him to a double homicide, all he had to do was head a short distance from where Nancy and Richard lived and toss the weapon into the dark waters of Lake Michigan. But the story did the trick of explaining how David ended up with the gun that killed Nancy and Richard under his bed. The question was, would the story stand up under cross-examination?

Now it was the prosecutor Pat O'Brien's turn to question David. O'Brien's tone was scornful as he asked why, in addition to having the gun, David also had a glass cutter, handcuffs, and burglary tools. Biro replied that he was fascinated with the crime and wanted to reenact it. Why the notebook with the press clippings and poem? O'Brien asked. Biro attributed that to the same thing: fascination with the crime and a desire to connect to it.

O'Brien dug deeper: why had David told classmates that he was the person who killed Nancy and Richard? Biro answered that he was only joking.

O'Brien shot back, incredulously, "What . . . about the Langerts pleading with you did you see the joke in? Where is the punch line?" David, unruffled until that moment, started to deflate on the stand. Watching it was excruciating in one way—David seemed to be literally squirming—and profoundly satisfying in another. O'Brien's obvious contempt for the answers he was getting stood in for my own.

David's testimony concluded with this exchange, when O'Brien was questioning David about having gone to Nancy and Richard's funeral:

MR. O'BRIEN:

Q You say you went to the funeral because you were compelled to do so because [this classmate] was a friend of yours and he had actually killed the Langerts, is that right?

A Yes.

Q But you weren't compelled at all to tell the Bishops, I know who killed your daughter and son-in-law, were you?

A No, I wasn't.

Q You were just compelled enough to go there and watch the Bishops suffer, weren't you?

A I wouldn't say that.

Q Well, did they look like they were having a good time?

MR. GEVIRTZ: Objection.

THE COURT: Sustained.

MR. O'BRIEN:

Q Did you see tears on Mrs. Bishop's face?

A I don't remember.

Q Did you see tears on Mr. Bishop's face?

A I don't remember.

Q Would it have mattered to you if you did?

A Possibly?

MR. O'BRIEN: Nothing further.

The rest of the trial was a blur. Two things I remember that haunted me. One was the moment when prosecutors held up the garments Nancy was wearing the night she died. Nancy loved clothes; she loved to shop and dress up. She looked beautiful, as she always did, during our celebration at the downtown restaurant on the last night she lived. The clothes she had picked out so carefully that night were torn by bullets and stiff with dried blood.

The other moment that stalked my dreams was this: prosecutors sought to introduce an autopsy photograph of the dead child in Nancy's womb. I could not see the picture; only the blank back of the large, blown-up photo was visible to spectators in the courtroom. But Bob Gevirtz could see it, and when he did, his face drained of color. Stricken, he told the judge it was the most inflammatory picture he had ever seen, and the jury should not view it. As an attorney, I have no doubt he was right. The judge agreed with him and excluded the picture.

I thought about it, though, the photograph of this baby whose tiny beating heart stopped when Nancy's life at last ebbed away. I wondered: was it a boy or a girl? The report of the autopsy didn't say, and the coroner who performed it couldn't remember. I felt sure I would see this child in heaven one day, but I longed to see it here, on earth. That baby would be a young man or woman in his or her twenties today, almost exactly the age Nancy was when she died.

The trial concluded on November 14, 1991, a little more than a week after it started. Jurors deliberated for only two hours before reaching a verdict. While they were cloistered in the airless conference room in the back, talking over the decision they would reach, I sat on the hard wooden bench in the courtroom, twisting my fingers and praying: *God, help them see the truth. Let them do the right thing.*

When they came back and the foreman of the jury spoke the word "guilty," I felt my jaw unlock, loosen, for what felt like the first time since the trial began. I looked at each of the jurors and silently told them with my eyes: *Thank you.* Then I looked at David Biro; his face was inscrutable, expressionless. No emotion, no outcry. It was as if he'd been expecting to hear that word: *guilty.*

The lawyers agreed to a continuance for posttrial motions and sentencing, and with that, the sheriffs took Biro away, back to the lockup. His walk, this time, was not the sauntering, cocky gait with which he had entered the courtroom that first day. He looked more subdued than threatening. The door separating the lockup from the courtroom swung shut behind him.

Done, I thought.

Months later, at Biro's sentencing, I sat beside my mother in the courtroom. Judge Shelvin Singer said words to this effect: I see a lot of young men coming into my courtroom with crimes like yours. But they are different from you. Most of them come from terrible childhoods, from abusive, broken homes and violent communities and a life of poverty. You didn't. You chose to do evil to an innocent young couple, for reasons I still can't understand.

Judge Singer pronounced the sentence: life in prison without the possibility of parole. As sheriffs led David away, my mother turned to me and said, "We'll never have to see him again."

We'll never see him again. I was glad of that. I fully expected it to be true.

After the sentencing, when my family and I walked out into the hallway, the press was waiting for us. We stood in a circle of cameras and reporters and spoke to them for the first time since the murders. One of the first things they wanted to know was this: Aren't you disappointed he didn't get the death penalty? (In Illinois at the time, there was a death penalty for adults, but not for people who committed murder as juveniles.

David, who killed when he was just one month short of legal adulthood, was ineligible for the sentence.)

I answered, speaking for myself only, since my mother and father were in favor of the death penalty as a general principle. I said no, I was not disappointed; I was relieved. The last thing I wanted was to widen the pool of bloodshed, dig another grave, create another grieving family. That wouldn't honor Nancy, who loved life. It wouldn't bring her back or assuage my grief. It would only cause another family to suffer as mine had. I wanted to prevent that, to draw a line that said this: the violence stops here, with me.

One reporter asked, if I didn't want the death penalty for David Biro, what did I want? I said I wished that part of his sentence would be that he would have to meet me face to face and answer my questions. *Why? Why Nancy and Richard?* That was something, I knew, that could never be. No court could force David Biro to speak with me, to give me the answers for which I longed.

I left the courthouse feeling more troubled than victorious. I had seen David Biro held accountable, brought to justice for taking the lives of my loved ones. The question was: what now? Locking him away forever was one response to what he had done. I knew it could not be the only response; there had to be more. If this day of sentencing were the end, it would be in a way the end of Nancy herself. If her voice didn't continue to speak somehow—if she didn't live on in some way other than my memory—it would be as if she had been wiped from the face of the earth, almost as if she had never existed at all.

A myth we families of murder victims often hear is this: that harsh sentencing of the perpetrator will bring "closure" for our grief. Sister Helen Prejean, Catholic nun, author of *Dead Man Walking,* and advocate for abolition of the death penalty, dismisses that idea. She told me once, "The word 'forgiveness' is problematic because it connotes 'forgive and forget.' One thing the victim's family never wants to do is forget."

Describing a gathering of victims' families in Oklahoma City after the 1995 bombing of the Alfred P. Murrah Federal Building that killed 168 people, Sister Helen said, "People were expressing their rage, wanting to participate in an execution. It gave them a focus and a lightning rod for their rage. People talked about the need for 'closure.' One man raised his hand and said, 'We lost a daughter. Could we just not use that word "closure" anymore? There will never be a night I don't miss her. You close on a house, or close the chapter of a book. You never close on a life.' "

It is true. What I longed for was not to have Nancy's life closed, but to have it be open—for Nancy's name to be remembered, and to have it propel me and the world toward something good and true and real.

Chapter 4

LEARNING CURVE

AFTER THE TRIAL, I FELT SOMETHING MISSING. I HAD GOTten what I'd hoped for—a conviction and life sentence for David Biro—but somehow it didn't seem enough. For the past year, ever since Biro's arrest for the murders, everything had pointed toward the moment when he would stand trial. Now that the trial was over, it left a gaping void. I was like a compass whose needle spins as it seeks a new direction.

I turned to the wisest man I knew, besides my dad: Dr. John Boyle, a pastor at my church and the founder of a counseling center attached to the church. John, as a young sergeant in the U.S. Army during World War II, had helped liberate the Nazi concentration camp at Dachau. John had vowed from that day in 1945 to return home and do whatever was the opposite of the evil and carnage he had witnessed. He became a Presbyterian minister and devoted his career to pastoral counseling, a calling that brought him close to people who had suffered from loss, abuse, addiction, betrayal, and bereavement. There was something solid and comforting about his serious, lined face, his silver hair, his deep voice, the quality of stillness and reflection he conveyed.

I sat on a beige couch in his quiet, book-lined office and poured out my own struggle: I have done everything I can to hold the person who killed Nancy responsible. I thought this would end this dark chapter in my life, that I could move on without the burden of anger and grief. Why do I feel that something is left undone? What do I do now?

John said, "Make a fist." I balled up my right hand into a knot. It felt like an echo of the exercise Reverend Buchanan had put me through more than a year ago, just after the murders.

"Now put it in front of your face," he said, demonstrating by placing his own fist within an inch of the bridge of his nose, right between his eyes. I did as he said.

"What do you see?" John asked.

I looked straight ahead, and all I could see, except for parts of John's office on the periphery, was my own hand, clenched before my eyes.

"I see a fist," I replied.

"Good," John said. "Now slowly, slowly, take that fist and move it down to your side." I gradually lowered my hand till it rested by my right thigh. "What do you see now?"

"I can see everything, the whole world," I answered.

"Do you see that fist," John asked, "the one that once blocked out everything else? It hasn't changed size or shape. It's just as big as it was before. It's just not *here*"—John raised his fist back to his face—"anymore.

"That fist is your grief over Nancy. It will be with you, the very same size and shape as it is now. Right now, it is blocking out the rest of the world. But over time, it will move away, down to your side. You will carry it alongside you while you walk. It just won't be *here*"—again, John held his fist to his face—"anymore."

I sat back in wonder. I recalled a friend's counsel that I needed to "get over" what had happened to Nancy; my mind had rebelled against that notion. I brought it up to John.

"You have had a loss," he responded. "You will never get over it. But you will get out from under it."

Relief coursed through me. I didn't have to reach that mythical state of "closure" after all! The memory of Nancy, the pain I felt upon losing her, my love for her—none of these were lost to me. John was telling me I could move ahead with that memory, love, and pain by my side as my companions.

Now I knew what to carry with me going forward. I also thought I knew what to leave behind: David Biro. From the moment the police told me that Nancy and Richard had been murdered, I sensed in my deepest core that hating the person who did it would affect him not a bit, but it would destroy me. I'd heard this saying: Hating someone is like drinking poison and expecting the other person to die. I refused to give him that power over me.

So I forgave David Biro. It didn't happen in an instant; rather, my forgiveness was an idea that gathered force over time, the way stones become an avalanche. One rock dislodged another, then another, till I felt my anger and rigidity giving way.

I forgave him, but it was the kind of forgiveness that wiped him off my hands like dirt. My forgiveness was not for David, who had gone through his arrest and trial without once taking responsibility or expressing remorse. He had not asked for forgiveness; he did not deserve it. My forgiveness was for God, for Nancy, and for me.

I left David behind, in the dust. God could deal with him. I vowed not even to speak his name; instead, I would go forward and think of Nancy, not him. It would be years before I realized that God wanted more from me.

Several years passed, and I began working in the juvenile division of the public defender's office, where I represented juveniles accused of committing a crime—some of them young men eerily resembling David Biro. The reminder unsettled me; every time I saw a tall, gangly teenager brought out of the lockup, part of me recoiled. I wanted to forget about him. God would not let me.

God's first unlikely messenger was an Indiana steelworker, Bill Pelke. Bill, a twenty-year crane operator for Bethlehem Steel, had heard about the murders in my family. He knew something of that: His grandmother, Ruth Pelke, had been killed in her own home, as Nancy was. A group of teenaged girls wanted money and decided to rob someone. They knew that Mrs. Pelke, a Sunday school teacher, would open her door to them. The ringleader, Paula Cooper, stabbed the elderly woman with a butcher knife thirty-three times. The thrusts were so vicious that the knife's blade plunged through Ruth Pelke's body and the carpet she lay on and chipped the wooden floor beneath. The girls took $10 and Ruth Pelke's car. Paula Cooper was fifteen years old.

At first, Bill had wanted the death penalty. He believed in executions. He thought his grandmother's death deserved the ultimate punishment. When the court sentenced Cooper to death by electrocution, he was satisfied. One night, though, he dreamed of his grandmother, a woman he still calls Nana. He could see her face. She was weeping. "I knew it was tears of love and compassion for this girl," Pelke told me, "and that Nana would want me to have love and compassion for her, too."

He started looking into Paula Cooper's troubled life and saw what led her to become the person who had knocked on Ruth Pelke's door. Paula Cooper had spent much of her childhood trying to run away from home, and for good reason: she was physically abused, and once was forced to watch the rape of her mother. Cooper was almost a murder victim herself—her mother had once allegedly tried to kill her. Bill joined the effort to get Cooper off death row. Her sentence was reduced to a term of years; she was released from prison in 2013 at age forty-three.

Bill had heard that I was looking for a way to honor Nancy's life. He was part of Murder Victims' Families for Reconciliation, an organization of victims' relatives who oppose the death penalty. They spoke and marched and lobbied against executions in places that had a death penalty. Their message was simple: don't kill in our names. Would I join the group?

I held up my palm to him. "The person who killed my family members has denied committing the crime. He's in effect saying to me, 'There's nothing to reconcile. There is no breach between us, because I have not wronged you.' How can I be part of a group about reconciliation?"

Pelke nodded sympathetically. He assured me that "reconciliation" meant only that I was not a barrier to the possibility of reconciling with one who has harmed me. "You are holding out a hand to him," Bill said. "It's up to him to take it."

Hulitt Gloer, Baptist seminary professor, pastor, and author, told me once, "We can't determine the response of the one we are forgiving. We can only say to him, 'What you did was unspeakable. You have left a hole in my heart that can never be filled. Yet, I forgive you.' He might choose to accept that forgiveness or to reject it. The bottom line here is not success; the bottom line is faithfulness."

So, cautiously, I joined Bill's group, and began to be asked to speak about forgiveness and the death penalty. The first invitation was to a gathering at the law school I had attended, Northwestern University School of Law. Perched on the lakefront in downtown Chicago, the school was hosting an event in support of Rolando Cruz, a man wrongfully convicted of killing a ten-year-old girl named Jeanine Nicarico. In 1983, the child had been at home sick on a school day, alone, when an intruder came to her door and abducted her.

Her small body was found two days later along a prairie path. She had been raped and sodomized before she was murdered. Cruz was in custody at the time of the law-school event; his execution date had been set, even though mounting evidence pointed to his innocence. (Cruz was twice convicted of the murder; the Illinois Supreme Court twice reversed those convictions. In 1995, he was tried a third time and acquitted after a prosecution witness recanted critical testimony. In 2002, Cruz was formally pardoned by Illinois Governor George Ryan. The outcry over Cruz's wrongful conviction eventually led to the indictment of three prosecutors and four police officers on charges of obstruction of justice, and his case played a large role in the abolition of the death penalty in Illinois.)

A series of prestigious people took the stage and spoke: lawyers, academics, and the former boxer Rubin "Hurricane" Carter, who had been wrongfully convicted of a 1966 triple homicide. Freed in 1985, Carter was the subject of the 1999 film *The Hurricane,* starring Denzel Washington. As I watched these polished speakers, nerves roiled my stomach. I ducked into the women's restroom and stared in the mirror. *What am I doing?* I asked the reflected image.

This story of Nancy and Richard, so precious to me, was something I had never shared publicly before. I had no confidence in myself as a speaker, but I believed in the power of that story. Telling it for something greater than myself, in an effort to save a human life— that, I could do. I looked in the mirror and nodded, *Go.*

When my turn to speak came, I stepped to the podium on the darkened stage. I spoke quietly but determinedly.

I told the story of Nancy and Richard's murder, and of how survivors of victims of violent crime often have a fantasy about how we could have rescued our loved ones. Mine was this: Instead of going back to my apartment after the dinner with Nancy and Richard on the night they died, I ride back with them to their home in Winnetka. Nancy and Rich walk through the front door; I am standing behind them. I glimpse in the dim light the killer waiting for them inside. As he points the gun at them, I run around to the back entrance to catch him by surprise. I pick up an object and bash him in the head with it. Nancy and Richard live.

"I didn't know that Nancy and Richard would die that day," I told the assembled crowd, "or I would have fought to save them. But we know the date and place and time that Rolando Cruz is scheduled to die. We can try to stop it. I am on my knees to the people in this room, because you don't have to care. But I do. I have to try to save a life, in memory of the ones I couldn't save. I will raise my one voice and say no to more killing."

Applause erupted, startling me. I stumbled off the stage and was greeted first by Rubin Carter, who grasped both my hands in his. "You could be bitter," he said, smiling exuberantly. "But bitterness consumes the vessel that contains it. Look at you! You are soaring!"

Andrea Lyon, a legendary criminal defense lawyer known as the Angel of Death Row for never having had a single one of her many clients sentenced to death, came up afterward. A tall, striking woman with a mane of long reddish-brown hair, Andrea fixed me with a steady gaze and said simply, "Thank you."

"For what?" I responded.

"For helping people like me not feel bad about what we do," she answered.

Feel bad? I wondered. *For saving lives?* Her grace and humility stunned me.

Not everyone was so supportive of my views on forgiveness and the death penalty. A few months later, a red-haired woman who heard me speak at a church approached afterward and said, "You must not have loved your sister very much."

"I'm sorry?" I replied, not sure I'd heard her correctly.

"You must not have loved her if you can forgive the person who killed her. Because I love my brother, and I would never, ever forgive anyone who took his life."

Worse was my experience when I testified at clemency hearings for prisoners on Illinois' death row.

It was an awful day. I had just had a miscarriage and was still bleeding, literally and figuratively. Someone had asked me to come to the opening day of mass hearings before the Illinois Prisoner Review Board for all the prisoners on death row. (The death penalty was still in force in Illinois at the time.) Then-Governor George Ryan was considering commuting the death sentences of those prisoners to life without parole because of the appalling rate of wrongful convictions in Illinois' death-row cases. One out of every two prisoners facing execution had been released based on actual innocence.

I hesitated, but agreed to come when I was assured that it would just be twenty minutes or so of speaking to the press. I didn't feel strong enough, physically or emotionally, to do more than that. I felt weak in body and shattered in heart, mourning the baby I had wanted, a little brother or sister for the young son I already had.

I donned a blue suit and headed to the State of Illinois Building on Chicago's venerable LaSalle Street for what I thought would be a short stint. Once I got there, someone greeted me and showed me my schedule for the day. I was to testify at one hearing in the morning and another in the afternoon.

"*Testify?*" I said, taken aback. Perhaps I had agreed to it, a long time before, and forgotten. But I knew this: I wasn't prepared to testify. I stared at the sheet of paper my handler had given me. My name was typed in two places, listing me as a witness in two hearings. The one in the morning was for Latasha Pulliam. The one in the afternoon was for the Mahaffey brothers.

Latasha Pulliam had been convicted of abducting a six-year-old girl, Shenosha Richards, from her South Side Chicago neighborhood. At Pulliam's apartment, she and her boyfriend sexually tortured the little girl, then Pulliam used a hammer to bash in the girl's skull and strangled her with an electrical cord. She tossed the little girl in a trash can, where her mother later discovered her.

Shenosha Richards's mother, testifying at the hearing, pled with the Prisoner Review Board not to let Pulliam out of her death sentence. If you commute her sentence to life, the mother said, that won't be the end of it; it will be only the beginning. My daughter's killer will keep trying to get out, and then someday I will walk down the street and see her, free. Shenosha's mother turned to the family of Latasha Pulliam and said how sorry she was for them, but she had to insist on execution. No one in that room could argue with her, not even the family members of the perpetrator. I could see them bowing their heads in resignation.

Then it was my turn, to speak for a commutation to a life sentence for Pulliam. I could barely choke out the words about the value of a human life, the grace of mercy, the importance of acting out of our own sense of morality rather than a desire for vengeance. I struggled with those words, after the gut-wrenching details I had just heard. But I said them, praying that the people in that hearing room might believe them, too. I looked at the mother of Shenosha Richards, her eyes deep pools of pain, and thought, *We should all be on our knees to this mother, begging her forgiveness. We promised her something we never should have: that we would kill for her, in response to the gruesome killing of her child. She is paying the price for that promise now, for our wrong.*

The afternoon, unbelievably, was worse. The Mahaffey brothers, Jerry and Reginald, had been convicted of breaking into the apartment of a young couple, Jo Ellen and Dean Pueschel, and their eleven-year-old son Richard. They raped and sodomized Jo Ellen and beat and stabbed her to death in the presence of her son. The Mahaffeys stabbed and beat the boy and his father, too, but succeeded in killing the father only. The boy managed to make it out of the apartment to an alley, where his grandfather found him. (The boy lived to grow up to be a police officer in a city near Chicago.)

The son's agony didn't end there: because one of the killers, Reginald Mahaffey, represented himself at a retrial of the case, Richard Pueschel had to be cross-examined on the stand by one of the very men who had murdered his parents. To add further insult to the injured family, the Mahaffey brothers had participated in an armed escape from the Cook County Jail while awaiting trial for the murders. Reginald was captured on jail grounds; Jerry was apprehended two days later.

The slain couple's family members were livid at the prospect that the two men might avoid death themselves if their sentences were commuted. They were furious at me for speaking for the Mahaffey brothers, at some points during the hearing turning around to glare at me and another person testifying against the death penalty for the Mahaffeys, the revered attorney and law professor Larry Marshall.

A relative of one of the victims, a woman with short blond hair, spoke at the hearing in a voice quivering with rage: "I wake up every morning and ask, *why are these two men still breathing?*" Her face bright red, she went on to reveal that she could no longer utter the Lord's Prayer. She could not say the words about being forgiven as we forgive those who have sinned against us, because, she said, "I will *never* forgive them."

It was heartbreaking. I looked at her as she took her seat, tense with anger, and I wondered, *What are the chances that those two men are waking up in prison every day thinking about you? They are locked up, but they have you in a prison, too. You cannot even say the prayer of your faith that you learned as a child; they have taken that from you, too.*

The atmosphere in the hearing room felt like a tsunami of hate. The air was suffused with it. How could I counter it, stand against that wave? When it came time for me to testify, I felt the assurance given in Luke 12:11–12: "When they bring you before . . . the authorities, do not worry about how you are to defend yourselves or what you are to say; for the Holy Spirit will teach you at that very hour what you ought to say."

I started talking about love. How much the family of the Pueschels clearly loved them. My sister Nancy's final message of love in her own blood. The promise of Scripture, that love is stronger than death. No evil the Mahaffeys could do, I argued, could be stronger than that love. A criminal sentence based on hatred and revenge would do nothing to honor the Pueschels or to reflect what their lives were about. My words felt puny and weak in the face of the momentous rage of the victims' families. I looked at the members of the Prisoner Review Board who sat, stone-faced, listening, and knew I was getting nowhere. The wave of hatred engulfed me and swept my words away.

When I was done, I glanced at the clock: it was past 7 p.m. The hearings had gone on all day and into the night.

It took every bit of composure I had not to cry as I left the hearing room. I held my head up as I walked through a gauntlet of press, prosecutors, and victims' family members who averted their eyes in disgust as I went by. I stepped out alone into the cold darkness. I managed to wait till I got into the cab I had hailed, then burst into tears. The cabdriver glanced in his rearview mirror, alarmed. I could not tell him why; I could only say, through clenched teeth, "I don't want to do this anymore. *I don't want to do this anymore!*"

It was a mantra I repeated all the way home, where I sat at my kitchen counter and worked my way through a bottle of Chardonnay. (I told this later to my friend Larry Marshall, who had testified as well. He said he had gone straight to a Mexican restaurant and done the same thing with a bottle of tequila.) A friend called to check on me. I wailed to her, "I don't want to do this anymore!"

"Jeanne," she said patiently. "Was what you did today wrong?"

The question startled me; I had to think for a minute. I hadn't asked for freedom for the people who had committed the sickening crimes I'd been hearing about all that day. I had only asked for life, for mercy. That was not wrong. "Nooooo . . . ," I answered, hesitantly.

"Well, all right then," she replied.

The truth is this: I felt more kinship with the mother of Shenosha Richards, with the son of Jo Ellen and Dean Pueschel, than I did with the killers of their loved ones. I felt an antipathy toward David Biro similar to the one they felt toward Latasha Pulliam and the Mahaffey brothers. I understood the revulsion, the desire to put this person away from you forever.

Building a high wall of separation between ourselves and those who have wronged us—that "putting away"—is meant to set ourselves apart, to relieve us from engaging with the wrongdoer. I did that.

I had forgiven David, yes, but it was forgiveness from a safe and tidy distance. I never told David Biro himself. Never wrote to him, never asked his lawyers or his family for a meeting. I was like Saul, the zealous, righteous one, in the book of Acts, before he encounters Jesus and is given a new name, Paul. I did not know that my road-to-Damascus moment was soon to come.

Chapter 5

KAIROS

MORE THAN A DECADE WENT BY. I HAD A SECOND SON, just days before my father died of the cancer he had endured so bravely. I carried my new baby in my arms, a little more than a week old, at my father's funeral. We stood in the November chill in front of the ivy-covered wall in the memorial garden where Nancy, Richard, and their baby were buried; my father was to be laid there beside them. A trumpeter played taps, elegant and austere. I looked down at the sleeping infant nestled against me and silently promised that he would know about his aunt and uncle, cousin and grandfather, resting in this place.

I became more active in the movement—in my state, in the nation, and across the world—to abolish

executions. In fall 2010, an invitation came to attend
a conference sponsored by People of Faith Against the
Death Penalty, a North Carolina–based organization
of people from a variety of faith traditions. The conference was to be held in Atlanta, partly at the historic
Ebenezer Baptist Church, where the Rev. Dr. Martin
Luther King Jr. had been a pastor. The title of the conference was "Kairos."

I looked up that word, *kairos*: it meant a turning
point, a propitious moment for decision or action. I had
no idea then that it would be exactly such a moment for
me, one in which I would cross paths with someone
who would change everything.

The conference speakers were a collection of lumi-
naries: Sister Helen Prejean, Catholic nun and author
of *Dead Man Walking*, the book upon which a play, an
opera, and an Oscar-winning film are based. The pastor of Ebenezer Baptist Church, the Rev. Dr. Raphael
Gamaliel Warnock. Stacy Rector, Presbyterian minister, head of Tennesseans for Alternatives to the Death
Penalty.

As I read the biographies of the presenters, two
people stood out. One was David Saperstein, a rabbi,
lawyer, and Jewish leader. His résumé was dazzling.
Saperstein worked at the intersection of faith and politics; I could learn a lot from him. The other was a law
professor from University of St. Thomas School of
Law in Minnesota named Mark Osler. He looked emi-
nently qualified to talk about faith and the death penalty. A graduate of the College of William and Mary
and Yale Law School, Osler had taught criminal law
for a decade at Baylor Law School in Waco, Texas, the

heart of death penalty country. He was the head of the Association of Religiously Affiliated Law Schools. He had written a book, *Jesus on Death Row,* challenging the death penalty based on the experience of Christ as a criminal defendant. His interviews and articles had appeared in hundreds of outlets: newspapers, radio, broadcast news, blogs, and law reviews.

All of that was impressive, but what struck me most about him was this: he was an ex-prosecutor. For five years, he had prosecuted federal crimes as an assistant U.S. attorney with the U.S. Department of Justice in his hometown, Detroit. He left that job and, from the look of his biography, had been working for mercy ever since. As lead counsel in a case before the U.S. Supreme Court, he won a decision ruling that sentencing judges could categorically reject the 100-to-1 sentencing ratio for crack to powder cocaine, which disproportionately punished minorities and the poor. The Samuel Goldwyn film *American Violet* depicted Osler's work with a former student to correct injustices perpetrated by Texas prosecutors. He was a prominent opponent not only of the death penalty but also of juvenile life without parole, testifying before the U.S. Congress against the sentence.

Who is this guy, this former prosecutor who is against the death penalty, who advocates for mercy? I wondered. I circled his name and Saperstein's on the program materials and made a mental note to try to meet them or, at the very least, hear them speak.

I succeeded with Saperstein, who was brilliant. I failed with Osler, though: his talks took place at times when I was meeting with other people. That was due to the main reason I'd wanted to attend the conference: I was going mostly to do one-on-one interviews for a writing project I was working on about faith and the death penalty.

The Kairos conference was a perfect opportunity to do this, a gathering of many of the people I'd wanted to talk to on the subject. They were a fascinating array:

Renny Cushing was a state representative in the New Hampshire legislature and the family member of two murder victims. Cushing's father, Robert, was shot to death in front of his wife in his home in Hampton, New Hampshire, by an off-duty police officer with a grudge against Cushing's family. Years later, Cushing's brother-in-law Stephen McRedmond was murdered by his nephew in Nashville, Tennessee, in eerily similar circumstances: on the front steps of his home, in front of his spouse. Cushing founded Murder Victims' Families for Human Rights (MVFHR), an organization of family members of homicide victims, including families of people executed by state or federal government. The group's board has included Robert Meeropol, who was orphaned when his parents, Julius and Ethel Rosenberg, were electrocuted by the United States as spies in 1953, and Bill Babbitt, whose brother Manny, a former Marine and recipient of the Purple Heart, was executed by the state of California for the murder of a seventy-eight-year-old woman after he returned from war.

Delbert Tibbs was a former seminary student in Chicago who had been traveling in Florida when two white hitchhikers were attacked by a black man who had stopped to pick them up. The woman was raped and her male companion was shot to death. Police arrested Tibbs for the crime; an all-white jury sentenced him to life for the rape and death for the murder. Two years later, the Florida Supreme Court reversed his conviction and the state dropped charges for lack of evidence. Tibbs became a poet and the basis for a character in the acclaimed play *The Exonerated*. The 2002 play told the stories of six people, all of them wrongfully convicted and nearly executed. The script was assembled from court documents, testimony, depositions, and letters, with Tibbs's graceful words shining through.

Bud Welch was a gas station owner in Oklahoma City whose only daughter, Julie Marie, age twenty-three, was killed in the bombing of the Murrah Federal Building by Timothy McVeigh in 1995. The blast killed 167 other people, including nineteen small children. Welch at first wanted the death penalty for McVeigh, then changed his mind. Welch realized that McVeigh's motivation for killing was revenge, and that the death penalty would only perpetuate the cycle of violence and retaliation. Welch tried unsuccessfully to visit Timothy McVeigh before he was executed, and did visit with McVeigh's father and sister. "I wanted to tell them, 'I don't hate your son. I don't hate you for what he did,' " Bud told me. Bud travels the world lobbying against the death penalty.

Marietta Jaeger's seven-year-old daughter, Susie, was abducted and murdered by a stranger when Marietta's family was on a camping trip in Montana. Marietta tucked her daughter in one night and woke to find a slit in the tent where Susie had lain. The child was gone. Her stuffed animals were strewn on the ground.

"It was clear something terrible had happened," Marietta recounted later, in a speech at the conference. Law enforcement searched for the little girl, bringing in the military, conducting sweeps of local suspects, recruiting people with small planes to join the search, dragging the river. Months went by with no sign of Susie and no arrests.

"I could see the toll this was taking on the rest of my kids. I could see the anguish in my husband's eyes. That was the day I got in touch with my rage," Marietta said. "I thought, what would I do if he were caught, what would I do to him? I imagined it all day long, and by the time I went to bed that night, I knew what I could do: I could kill him with my bare hands and a smile on my face." As she turned to go to sleep, she could hear a voice inside her, the voice of God, saying, "But that's not how I want you to feel."

Marietta said, "I knew that God was calling me to forgive this person, but I wasn't ready. I struggled and argued my stance. I struggled and wrestled with God. But who wins when you struggle with God? I knew if I gave myself to this rage and desire for revenge, it would consume me. I gave God permission to change my heart. That was the first night I had a good night's sleep.

"I was aware something incredible was happening to me. I saw that in God's eyes, he was just as precious as my little girl. He was a son of God. Jesus died for him, too. He had dignity and worth."

Marietta began to do something that she probably never dreamed she'd do: she began to pray for the person who had taken Susie, whoever he was. She prayed, unbelievably, that good would come to him.

Her prayers for her daughter's abductor were very specific: If his car broke down by the side of the road, that someone would stop to help him. If he went fishing, that he would catch a lot of fish. "The more I prayed for him, the more I realized how important it was to have God in his life. Because if he had Susie, I wanted him to be good to her, and if she was dead, I wanted him to come forward and tell me what happened."

When Marietta told that story to the audience at the conference, I shook my head as I listened. *I could never do that*, I thought. Pray for good to come to this person? Never. She is on a plane higher than one I could ever attain. It is otherworldly.

About a year after Susie was kidnapped, her abductor telephoned Marietta, taunting her. She kept him on the phone long enough that he could be tracked; the call led to his capture. After that arrest, Marietta learned that he had killed Susie only a short time after he had pulled the sleeping child from her tent. He had taken her to an abandoned farmhouse and locked her in a broom closet. Every day, he left her in the small closet, naked in her own excrement. Every night, he brought her food and water and raped her. Within weeks of her abduction, he strangled the little girl to death and dismembered her body. The killer's name was also David. David Meirhofer.

After Meirhofer's arrest, Marietta advocated for a life sentence in prison rather than the death penalty. Because she was not seeking execution, Meirhofer agreed to plead guilty to a life sentence for the crime. He did not live to serve that sentence: he took his own life the same day he pled to the murders of Susie and three other victims. Marietta speaks in prisons now, to inmates. One such speech, at a prison in Montana, left many of the grown men in the audience in tears. (Marietta wrote to me after that experience, "Yay, Susie!")

On the first afternoon of the Kairos conference, Renny, Bud, Marietta, and I went to Ebenezer Baptist Church for a press conference. We were all to go to dinner afterward. They were onstage for the press conference; I sat alone in a pew in the back of the church. A small group of people sat in front of me, including some I didn't know. We all were wearing name tags, with our first names in large letters and our last names in small print.

One of the people in the pew ahead of me was a man in his forties with brown curly hair and a tweed jacket. He was looking down at his phone, scrolling for messages, returning some. He looked very important and very busy. I peered at his name tag; I could see the large first name, "MARK."

I leaned forward in my pew to speak to him. "I haven't met you yet. I'm Jeanne Bishop. What is your last name?"

"Osler," he said, turning around to meet my gaze. His face was kind.

"You're Mark Osler!" I exclaimed. "I read about you. I wanted to hear your talk."

"Did you?" he replied.

"No," I confessed. "I missed it. But I heard it was great." It was true. Others had told me Osler's speech was a passionate rant, which began in a methodical and scholarly fashion and crescendoed into a kind of call-and-response with the audience.

Osler looked at me with what seemed like patient amusement as I explained who I was—part of a group of murder victims' family members—and what I was doing there. I invited him to come to dinner with us. On the way to the bus that would take us to the restaurant, I introduced him to Renny, Bud, and Marietta. Politely, Osler asked what my connection was to them. It was too much to put into words: my sister Nancy, Renny's father Robert, Bud's daughter Julie, Marietta's little girl, Susie. "These are my people," I answered, without further explanation. That was true, too; they were. Somehow, I sensed Osler would get it.

As we parted after dinner that night, I observed that Osler and I were both unlikely opponents of the death penalty, he a former prosecutor and me the loved one of murder victims. "You know the grief of loss, and I know the weight of judgment," he said quietly.

He reached into his briefcase and handed me something: his book, *Jesus on Death Row*. It was a slim, elegant volume with a black cover bearing a striking image: Jesus' crown of thorns, except instead of thorns it was composed of the steel razor wire one sees looped at the top of prison fences.

I read his book on the plane on the way back to Chicago. I was riveted. Why had no one thought of this before? The book's central thesis was this: The Gospels' story of Jesus is, in large part, the story of his arrest, detention, trial, and execution. That was purposeful, not accidental. The conclusion is inescapable: God intended Christ to come to earth not just as a teacher, preacher, and healer. God also intended Jesus to be a criminal defendant, a man who was held—albeit briefly—on the death row of his time. If that is so, what are we to conclude about Jesus? About prisoners? About the death penalty?

Painstakingly, Osler's book takes the reader through the process of a modern criminal arrest, legal proceedings, and execution, and compares it, step by step, with what Jesus experienced. He addresses head-on those who would take offense at Jesus being compared to modern-day death-row prisoners, most of whom are murderers, noting that Christ himself invited us to do exactly that. Osler points out that Jesus specifically compared visiting people in prison to visiting him ("I was hungry and you gave me food, I was thirsty and you gave me something to drink, I was a stranger and you welcomed me, I was naked and you gave me clothing, I was sick and you took care of me, I was in prison and you visited me," Matt. 25:35–36). Osler writes,

> I have no problem with equating the hated, the guilty, even the imprisoned and reviled killer with Christ, for it is at Christ's invitation that I compare my society's treatment of "the least of these" with that of Christ himself. (p. 6)

I leaned forward in my airplane seat and pulled a pen from my purse. I started underlining passages and writing notes in the margins as I read. One chapter that struck me compares a condemned man's last meal to the Last Supper of Christ before his execution, and observes that the meal is our common touch point: both the hand of the murderer and the hand of Christ take the bread. Osler writes:

We are somewhere in between the Savior and the killer. We exist in that wide chasm between the murderer and Christ, yet our common experience meets the murderer in the precise place where it meets the life of Christ. There is an elegant symmetry between the Christ who is perfect beyond our comprehension and the murderer who is flawed beyond our comprehension, and their experiences are like ours in only the most basic of ways. As the murderer picks up the bread, so did Christ, and so do we. Though Christ and the murderer come from opposite directions, something inside us compels us to try to understand both, and in that attempt to understand we are pulled toward those few brief moments when we share something like the feeling of bread in our hands.

Food—that, we understand. (p. 67)

I finished the book just as the wheels of the plane touched down at O'Hare Airport. I had been so immersed, I'd barely noticed time passing until we bumped onto the ground. I held the book in my hand, thinking, *this is something startling, deep and true.* As my plane taxied to the gate, I tucked the book into my purse, pulled out my phone, and sent a one-sentence message to Mark Osler: *I love your book.*

It upended the way I saw my work as a public defender. If Matthew 25 is to be believed, then the prisoners I represented were not just ordinary, sometimes difficult men and women. They were not a problem to be solved. They were Jesus. Their mothers, who came to court and flagged me down in hallways, and sometimes berated me for not doing enough to help their child, were all Mary, the mother of Jesus.

Osler's book did more than that: it shook up the way I thought about the most significant prisoner in my life, David Biro. Until that moment, I would have thought it impossible to compare Jesus and Biro in any way. David Biro had broken into the home of a happy young couple and killed their dream when he killed them. His acts were evil. What connection could there be between him and Jesus, the Prince of Peace? And yet, I knew Osler was right: Jesus was asking me—all of us—to see in the face of David Biro the face of Christ himself.

This cold-blooded killer as Jesus? My mind rebelled at the very possibility—but I could feel a nudging, a door, long bolted, starting to be pushed open.

We often imagine it is the world that changes us—someone gets elected, or a sports team wins, or we get a new job, and things will be better or worse for us. Really, though, it is usually ideas that change us; the book in our lap may be more important than anything else. We hear a story, we read about a life well lived, and the earth shifts subtly beneath us, the Holy Spirit breathes in our ear. It changes us—in ways that we never could have expected—and then we change the world, if only the small part of it within the reach of our own two hands.

Chapter 6

THE GIFTS

THAT BOOK WAS ONLY THE FIRST OF MANY GIFTS MARK Osler would give me, gifts that challenged my assumptions, cracked open the hard shell of my certainty, and made me see things in a startlingly new way.

The second gift was a person.

Osler, knowing my interest in the topic, sent me the book *Forgiveness: Christian Reflection* (Center for Christian Ethics at Baylor University, 2001). It contained a chapter by Dr. Randall O'Brien, Mark Osler's friend and former colleague at Baylor University. O'Brien had left Baylor to become president of a Baptist college in Tennessee. A minister and author, O'Brien had an intriguing personal history. Born and raised in Mississippi, he had volunteered for the U.S. Army and served two tours of duty in Vietnam, during which he must have seen brutality similar to that which John Boyle witnessed during World War II. He went on to attend Yale Divinity School and to teach and preach at a host of other prestigious institutions.

I read O'Brien's chapter about forgiveness and thought it was wonderful, until I got to this sentence: "No Christian is ever in the position of privilege, wronged one or wrongdoer, where he or she is excused from the responsibility of working for reconciliation" (p. 20).

I skidded to a halt. *What??* I thought, indignant. This was asking too much. I had forgiven Nancy's killer. I had not reconciled with him because I *couldn't.* He had denied responsibility for his crime. O'Brien was not only asking me to reconcile with this unrepentant killer; he was telling me I was *obligated to work for* that reconciliation.

The next morning, I called Mark Osler to vent. Sitting in a grocery store parking lot, cell phone clasped to my ear, I complained loudly about this sentence that had so affronted me, this notion that victims must try to reconcile with unrepentant offenders. How could Randall O'Brien suggest such a thing?

Mark said, "Why don't you call Randall and ask him?"

"I can't call a college president and complain about something he wrote!" I shot back.

"Yes, you can," Mark replied. "I know Randall. He will be very gracious and say something loving, and then he will tell you the truth."

I asked for O'Brien's phone number; Mark gave it to me.

"One other thing you should know," he said, as I scratched the number on an envelope. "Randall sounds exactly like Jimmy Carter."

It took days to gather the nerve to dial that number, to the Office of the President of Carson-Newman College (now University). When I finally did, O'Brien was out; his assistant took a message. I waited to hear back, wondering if he would return a phone call from a stranger.

The call came as I was sitting in my car, heater on full blast, in an icy, windswept parking lot at O'Hare Airport. I was waiting to pick up a friend, alone in my car, in the midst of a desolate sea of concrete. "Jeanne Bishop?" said a genial, lilting voice on the phone. Osler was right: he did sound like Jimmy Carter!

I turned down the loud heater in my car and launched in, explaining why I wanted to speak with him. O'Brien listened carefully as I told the story of Nancy's murder. Snow swirled outside my car and settled onto earth that looked made of iron. I imagined him on the other end, in Jefferson City, Tennessee, where already green shoots would be springing up from ground that was soft and warm.

I asked him my question: how can I reconcile with someone who has never admitted his guilt or expressed remorse?

O'Brien demurred. He did exactly what Mark Osler told me he would do: instead of answering right away, he showered me with love. He told me that I was far down the road of faith already, farther than him. Undaunted, I pressed for an answer. In an affable voice, he told me I sounded like a deeply faithful Christian and an intelligent person who would be able to figure out the answer for herself.

"No," I persisted. "Tell me what trying to reconcile with someone who isn't sorry would even look like!"

He paused, then said simply, "It would look like Jesus on the cross."

Tears started in my eyes. He did not need to say the words. I knew what they were: *Father, forgive them.* . . .

Randall went on, his voice picking up intensity, saying this: We are all murderers. We are all responsible for the death of the sinless Son of God. We all crucified him. On that, there is no distinction between you and your sister's killer. Both of you were made in the image of God; God loves you both. What did Jesus do on the cross while he was being murdered? He prayed for those who were murdering him at the very moment they were in the act of killing him.

Wouldn't it be amazing, Randall asked, if God used you to bring this young man into relationship, if he joined you in heaven one day?

I felt my heart, hard and rigid, cracking open. I had always made a divide between Nancy's killer and me. Him: bad murderer. Me: innocent victims' family member. The truth was that we were the same; there was no division between us before God. We were both flawed and fallen. We were both God's children. I could no longer draw a line between us that put me on one side and him on the other.

Pray for David Biro? I had never even thought of praying for him. The shame of it cut me to the heart.

Not only had I never prayed for him; I had never even spoken his name.

In the years after Nancy died, when I worked against the death penalty, for gun violence prevention, for forgiveness, I never once mentioned the name of her killer. I did that on purpose: I wanted his name to die and Nancy's and Richard's to live. I wanted the world to remember Nancy and Richard and to forget him. The last thing I wanted for him was the notoriety of a John Wayne Gacy or a Jeffrey Dahmer. I wanted him to fade into obscurity. That is not uncommon for victims' families; we resist anything that turns our loved ones' murderers into celebrities. That rewards evil rather than punishing it. We want for the killers not fame, but anonymity.

My strategy had worked. People who heard Nancy and Richard's story remembered their names and not the name of their killer. That felt like a kind of victory to me.

I'd wanted to bury this young man in the sands of time. Randall was suggesting that I do the opposite: lift him up to God, pray for his redemption. The David Biro he was asking me to envision was a David Biro reclaimed, brought home in the embrace of God.

That sounded utterly preposterous to me, impossible, even. It was inconceivable that prayer could do something as radical and life-changing as to turn a coldhearted murderer into a follower of God. To bring him into relationship with the family of the woman he'd killed. But implicit in Randall's challenge to me was this: with God, nothing is impossible.

Do I really believe that? I asked myself. I knew that if I called myself a Christian, I had to believe it. I had staked my life on it. Jesus said, "Follow me," and I had some idea what that meant: Follow him to the marginalized, to the despised. Follow him to miracles, to the cross, to the empty tomb, to all that baffles and confounds us. God cannot be contained by the limits of human understanding; God is more vast and powerful, and loving and gracious, than our minds can grasp. God calls us to risk everything, to venture out from our comfortable places in faith and courage—to give our lives away, and thereby to find them.

The next day, I woke early with this thought: how can I pray for someone whose name I will not even utter? Isn't rendering him nameless akin to making him a nonperson? I thought about calling Randall back to ask him, then laughed. I could hear his voice in my head, speaking in his Southern drawl, "If you are asking the question, you already know the answer." I did.

So, I told myself I would repent. I would speak the name of the man who'd killed my sister. I would take the first step.

Mark Osler gave me the opportunity to act on my repentance, his third gift to me, fittingly enough during the season of Lent.

He was putting Jesus on trial, something he had developed as a young law professor in Texas. He had noticed two things about the culture there: most people publicly identified themselves as Christians, yet strongly supported the death penalty. Osler was struck that those two things would go together, since at the heart of Christian faith is the story of an unjust execution. His idea: to juxtapose that story—the trial and death sentence of Jesus Christ—with modern death-penalty law in an unscripted courtroom drama performed live before an audience.

He had put Jesus on trial in a mock proceeding at the large Baptist church he had attended in Waco before an audience of congregants. Osler played the prosecutor; his Baylor colleague Bill Underwood played the defense attorney for Jesus. The law being applied was Texas's actual death-penalty law. Two of the congregants who acted as jurors were people who had served as forepersons of real Texas juries that had voted in favor of death for the defendant on trial.

Now, Osler had been asked to give a presentation on the death penalty at a friend's church in Virginia, the state second only to Texas in the number of people it has executed. Osler decided to resurrect the trial of Jesus and perform it at the church.

By this time, Bill Underwood had become a college president and could no longer portray the defense attorney for Jesus. Osler asked me to step in. "I figured Jesus was indigent. He would have needed a public defender," Osler explained.

The trial was scheduled to take place on the night before Palm Sunday, the same night of the year that Nancy and Richard were killed twenty-one years earlier. The trial would be conducted under Virginia law as if in a real death-penalty sentencing proceeding. We would give opening statements, call witnesses to testify, and make closing arguments. The audience would be our jurors. At the close of the trial we would ask the audience to decide on a sentence: Life in prison? Or execution?

The Church of the Holy Comforter in Richmond was, in its own quirky way, the perfect place to hold the trial. Outwardly, it is a stately Episcopal church, a brick edifice with a red door and lovely garden. Located on Richmond's historic Monument Avenue, a long street populated with statues of Confederate generals, the church appears genteel and placid.

Inside, though, the church—affectionately nicknamed Hoco by its members—is buzzing with energy and populated with an assortment of unforgettable characters, starting with the man who had invited us to the church. Tall, sandy-haired Craig Anderson is a counselor for a local college whose gentle manner belies his background as a bare-knuckles college hockey player from Boston.

The alchemy of that vibrant church turned Mark's idea to do the trial into a series of events, all focused on the death penalty. We had an evening discussion at the church before the trial as a kind of backdrop against which the trial would be held. Mark spoke about his reasons for opposing the death penalty, based on his Christian faith and his experience as a former prosecutor. I spoke, too, and when I did, I told the story of Nancy's murder, of the murderer, of Randall O'Brien and the book.

Heart in my throat, I did what we do in my Presbyterian church each Sunday at the start of worship: I publicly confessed. I told the people gathered there at Hoco that in the years since my sister's murder, I had never prayed for the killer or spoken his name.

I looked out at the hushed audience and said, "I am saying that name now: David Biro."

It felt strange to hear that name coming from my lips. It echoed through the vaulted sanctuary. As the sound of it faded in the air, I felt a burden lifting off of me. The weight of it! I hadn't known how heavy, till then.

Looking back at me in the soft glow of the lamp-lit church were the faces of people who had already become dear to me: Craig; his radiant wife, Lori; Steve and Peggy, stalwart Episcopalians and law reformers; Martha, the red-haired, pixieish music director for the church; Cameron, faithful volunteer. I felt enveloped in love—the love of the beloved gathered there, and the all-encompassing love of God.

I did pray for David. I went back home to Chicago that Lenten season and began in the only place I could, at the grave where Nancy and Richard and their baby are buried. It is inside a quiet walled garden beside the church where they were married. Their names are carved into an ivy-covered stone wall. Nancy Bishop Langert. Richard Alexander Langert. Baby Langert. A tree shades the place where they rest. I dropped to my knees and prayed for God to open my heart, to forgive me. I asked for peace and rest for Nancy and Richard. Then I asked for God's blessing on David Biro. I felt as if a stone had been rolled away from my heart.

The English word "Lent" comes from the German *lenz* and the Dutch *lente*. It means spring. I was starting to understand—this is what restoration means. It means the hard earth softening, green plants shooting up, buds opening, leaves unfurling. It means life bursting forth from dormant earth, the still, small voice of God remaking God's creation from within. For years, I had resisted; now, I could feel it happening to me.

Part 2

What Comes After

Chapter 7

DAVID

Who was David Biro, this person I was starting to pray for? I had to find out. As I began to learn about him, everything I discovered painted the portrait of a sociopath.

- One of Biro's high school counselors was a friend of a partner I had worked for at Mayer Brown. The counselor said, "Biro wasn't the worst kid I had. But he was the scariest. [If they did something wrong,] the other kids felt bad about what they had done. He didn't even understand why he should feel bad."
- Biro's psychiatric social worker from Charter Barclay described him as charming, manipulative, and utterly without empathy. In a conversation

years after the trial, the social worker told me that she had begged the Biro parents to return David to the institution for treatment when he skipped out after the weekend pass, but they refused. The social worker said she was horrified when she later read in the papers that David had committed murder; she said she had seen it coming—that he was capable of killing someone—and she had been helpless to prevent it.

– A former cell mate of David's wrote from prison to tell me that David had casually discussed the murders with him, expressing no remorse. When another high-profile, multiple murder occurred while they were in custody together—the shooting deaths of women shoppers at a local Lane Bryant store—one of the victims happened to have the same name as my older sister. The cell mate said David had hoped that it was she who had been killed.

– A lawyer acquaintance took me aside in court one day and revealed that he had been a high school classmate of David's at New Trier. Students then were allowed to go outside the building and smoke, and the two had spent some time smoking together between classes. "He was a strange kid, always wearing black, creepy sense of humor. He never talked about killing, but if you had asked me when he was arrested for murder if I was surprised, I would have said no."

How would I pray for this person? How should I think of him in the context of my Christian faith? I turned to the Bible and looked for people like him who had killed. They were easy to find—their names were familiar.

Moses took a human life.

Right after the tale of the infant Moses being lifted from a basket in the river and made a son of the Egyptian pharaoh's daughter, this story appears in the book of Exodus:

> One day, after Moses had grown up, he went out to his people and saw their forced labor. He saw an Egyptian beating a Hebrew, one of his kinsfolk. He looked this way and that, and seeing no one he killed the Egyptian and hid him in the sand. (Exod. 2:11–12)

Moses' murder was discovered; he became a fugitive and fled to another country.

David, king of Israel, ordered the death of an innocent man. David had sex with Bathsheba, the wife of a man who was away at war in David's service. When she became pregnant, Bathsheba sent a message giving David that news. He tried unsuccessfully to get the unsuspecting husband to come home from the battle and sleep with his wife, hoping that would hide David's role in the pregnancy. The faithful soldier, named Uriah, refused to do that as long as his fellow fighters were still in the field.

David then wrote a letter to the commander in the field and sent it by Uriah's own hand. The letter contained Uriah's death sentence: "Set Uriah in the forefront of the hardest fighting, and then draw back from him, so that he may be struck down and die" (2 Sam. 11:15). David's murderous plot succeeded; the innocent husband was killed in battle.

Saul sanctioned the slaughter of the earliest Christians, before God gave him a new name, Paul. The first Christian martyr, Stephen, was stoned to death for professing Jesus Christ. During that stoning, "the witnesses laid their coats at the feet of a young man named Saul" (Acts 7:58). "And Saul approved of their killing him" (Acts 8:1). Saul went on to unleash persecution against Christians in Jerusalem, "ravaging the church by entering house after house; dragging off both men and women" (Acts 8:3).

Moses, David, Paul. They killed, or aided and abetted killing, each of them. God didn't throw them away; God redeemed them and used them for good.

Moses led his people out of slavery in Egypt to freedom in a new land. David defeated enemies, established a kingdom, is thought to have written some of our most beloved psalms. Paul became an apostle of Christ who expanded the reach of the good news of the gospel throughout the first-century world.

They suffered, to be sure. Moses struggled through plagues and terror, hunger and thirst, wandering in the desert. He died before reaching the homeland God had promised. David's reign after Bathsheba was riddled with bloodshed and tragedy, including the death of the child Bathsheba conceived and the murder of another of David's sons, Absalom. Paul was arrested, beaten, flogged, shipwrecked, imprisoned, and martyred.

God restored them. Their restoration stories are echoed in the Gospel stories: Jesus cleansing lepers, calling tax collectors to his service, speaking to Samaritans, protecting an accused adulterer, healing people beset by what were called "demons." Jesus brought even the most marginalized back into community. He gave them new life.

Could David Biro be restored? Was he, like those figures in the Bible, capable of being touched and transformed by God? My mind could barely contain such a thought; it seemed as improbable as turning a monster into a man—fully sentient, driven by conscience.

David Biro seemed to me more like the first murderer recorded in the Bible: Cain.

That resonated because David Biro had specifically identified himself with Cain; he had signed that name to a poem he had written in the notebook police recovered from his bedroom:

> Remember that I am the second son of Adam and Eve.
> Remember that I rose up in front of God and slew my brother Abel out of greed.
> Remember it all, but if somehow you should forget some of it, just remember this: my name is Cain, and I kill people.

The story of Cain is told in the book of Genesis:

> Now Abel was a keeper of sheep, and Cain a tiller of the ground. In the course of time Cain brought to the LORD an offering of the fruit of the ground, and Abel for his part brought of the firstlings of his flock, their fat portions. And the LORD had regard for Abel and his offering, but for Cain and his offering he had no regard. So Cain was very angry, and his countenance fell. The LORD said to Cain, "Why are you angry, and why has your countenance fallen? If you do well, will you not be accepted? And if you do not do well, sin is

lurking at the door; its desire is for you, but you must master it."

Cain said to his brother Abel, "Let us go out to the field." And when they were in the field, Cain rose up against his brother Abel, and killed him. Then the LORD said to Cain, "Where is your brother Abel?" He said, "I do not know; am I my brother's keeper?" And the LORD said, "What have you done? Listen; your brother's blood is crying out to me from the ground! And now you are cursed from the ground, which has opened its mouth to receive your brother's blood from your hand. When you till the ground, it will no longer yield to you its strength; you will be a fugitive and a wanderer on the earth." Cain said to the LORD, "My punishment is greater than I can bear! Today you have driven me away from the soil, and I shall be hidden from your face; I shall be a fugitive and a wanderer on the earth, and anyone who meets me may kill me." Then the LORD said to him, "Not so! Whoever kills Cain shall suffer a sevenfold vengeance." And the LORD put a mark on Cain, so that no one who came upon him would kill him. (Gen. 4:2–15)

A bizarre story, and one which so perplexed me that I turned to one of the wisest people I know, law professor and Catholic spiritual director Susan Stabile, to help me understand it.

"Cain bears God's mark," Susan explained. "It means God is not disclaiming him. He still belongs to God. God is saying, 'You are still mine.' He is going to be punished, but God is not done with him."

God is not done with him. I knew in the next instant: God was not done with David Biro.

My two young sons helped me see that. One summer night, the three of us were walking from an outdoor concert in Chicago's Millennium Park, near the lakefront. The air was soft. Small black birds swooped overhead, silhouetted against the city's majestic sky-scrapers. The sun was going down, and at one point its evening rays must have glinted on my hair. My older son, Brendan, commented on this, wondering aloud when it would start to turn gray. I started telling them about my father, the grandfather they knew as Papa, who died at the age of seventy-four with a full head of blond hair, not a strand of white to be seen.

"Once when I asked Papa why he had never turned gray, he said it was because he had a pure heart," I said, smiling.

"A pure heart," Brendan, then age eleven, repeated. "What does that mean?"

"It means," I replied, "that you love the Lord your God with all your heart and all your soul and all your strength and all your mind, and your neighbor as yourself."

My younger son, Stephen, then age seven, immediately asked, "What about the person who killed Aunt Nancy?"

Stephen's question took me aback. How could this little boy so quickly put together these two ideas: that we are called to love our neighbor, and that one of our neighbors—David Biro—killed the precious aunt who died before Stephen was born? Marveling at my children, the depth of their thoughts, I hesitated to answer the question for them. "What do you think?" I inquired.

They thought about the question for a moment as we walked along, toting our picnic blanket. Then the older one, Brendan, said, "We can't love what he did, but we have to love him, because God made him for a purpose."

My jaw dropped. *God made him for a purpose.* That had never occurred to me. God had a purpose for David Biro. I wondered for the first time: what might that purpose be?

Chapter 8

CHANGE OF HEART

In the winter of 2012, months after an important Supreme Court decision on juveniles who had killed, I was talking with Mark Osler about a topic on which he is an expert, and over which we had clashed in the past: the sentence given to David Biro, juvenile life without parole.

A prominent advocate for lessening overly harsh criminal penalties, Osler has been a vocal opponent of natural life for juveniles. From television interviews on CNN to testifying before U.S. congressional committees on the subject, Osler has consistently called for an end to the sentence.

Me? I wasn't so sure.

I had come a long way since the day David got that sentence, years earlier. Then, I was glad he would be locked away forever. It meant I didn't have to think about him anymore. I was free to focus on the work I did in memory of Nancy. So I continued to support the possibility of life sentences for juveniles who had committed heinous murders.

Over time, though, I began to experience some doubts. I was troubled by the principled opposition to juvenile life sentences of friends I admired, people who were my moral compass, a kind of true north: Sister Helen Prejean, who argues that people are more than the worst act they have ever committed. Bernardine Dohrn, the now-retired Northwestern University law professor who moved from a turbulent past as part of the Weather Underground to a lifetime of advocacy on behalf of the legal rights of children. Randolph Stone, the man who had hired me at the public defender's office, champion of the rights of criminal defendants, with a special heart for the generation of young African American men who are incarcerated at a dramatically high rate.

I felt compelled to ask: *Am I wrong on this? Are they right?*

I felt the same when I met Osler; we agreed on every important criminal-justice issue except this one. We debated each other as opponents on radio, on television, and in front of the entire incoming class at his law school one year. Osler spoke about children and mercy. I spoke about justice and fear.

It felt terrible.

I wanted to believe I was right. I told myself that the hundred or so inmates in my state who were serving juvenile life sentences richly deserved to leave prison only in a coffin.

- Johnny Freeman, sixteen, lured a five-year-old girl to a vacant apartment on an upper floor of a Chicago public housing building. He raped her and pushed her out of a window. The little girl clung to the windowsill with her tiny fingers and screamed for her mother. Freeman walked to the window and pushed the child again, sending her plummeting fourteen stories to her death.
- Curtis Croft, sixteen, along with two codefendants raped a teenaged girl, then debated what to do with her. Should they give her something to eat and let her go? Or kill her? The three decided it would be better for them if she were dead. They made sure that happened: they laid her in a roadway and ran over her body five times with a car, then finished her off with forty stab wounds.

My reasoning for supporting life imprisonment for juvenile criminals like these was the following: if you do that, your depravity is so great that you've torn up the card that gives you a right to be out in society. The mothers of those girls, whose last moments were spent in pain and terror, have a right to go out in their neighborhoods and not see you walking free, ever.

I knew people like those mothers, family members of other victims murdered by juveniles, whom I'd met in the course of my work against gun violence and the death penalty.

- Dora Larson, whose ten-year-old daughter Victoria was lured into a field by a teenaged boy who had dug a grave there three days earlier. He raped and strangled her, then dumped her small body into the grave he had prepared for her. He was on probation for another offense at the time of his crime.
- Priscilla Pulido, whose younger brother, Ruben, age thirteen, was playing basketball in his driveway on a warm July night. Gangbangers who didn't even know him shot him to death, along with the thirteen-year-old friend playing ball with him.

What I had wanted—what those other family members wanted—was something equal to the magnitude of the lost lives of our loved ones. A precious, irreplaceable human being had been wiped off the face of the earth. Nothing but life imprisonment seemed big enough to match the enormity of that loss.

My belief in juvenile life sentences had support, too, from a variety of sources:

Academic. Beginning in the late 1980s, juvenile life sentences were widely adopted by state legislatures based on forecasts from academics such as Harvard professor James Q. Wilson, who (as Mark Kleiman wrote in "In Memoriam: James Q. Wilson," March 2, 2012, www .samefacts.com) posited the existence of "a new generation of 'juvenile super-predators,' whose propensity for violence put the nation at risk of a bloodbath once they became adults unless they were put behind bars." (Wilson later recanted that position.)

Legal. Four U.S. Supreme Court justices—John Roberts Jr., Clarence Thomas, Samuel Alito Jr., and Antonin Scalia—vigorously dissented in 2012 when the Court held 5–4 in a case called *Miller v. Alabama* that mandatory sentences of juvenile life without parole were an unconstitutional violation of the Eighth Amendment ban on cruel and unusual punishment. Writing for the dissenters, Chief Justice Roberts argued:

> Mercy toward the guilty can be a form of decency, and a maturing society may abandon harsh punishments that it comes to view as unnecessary or unjust. But decency is not the same as leniency. A decent society protects the innocent from violence. A mature society may determine that this requires removing those guilty of the most heinous murders from its midst, both as a protection for its other members and as a concrete expression of its standards of decency.

Psychological. In an article titled "Can You Call a 9-Year-Old a Psychopath?" (*New York Times Magazine*, May 11, 2012), Jennifer Kahn described a psychologist's study of "callous-unemotional" children who show a lack of remorse or empathy. One child described in the article, nine-year-old Jeffrey Bailey, pushed a toddler into the deep end of a Florida swimming pool. He pulled up a chair to watch as the child sank to the bottom. Bailey told police later that he wanted to see someone drown. He was described as happy to be the center of attention and unfazed by the possibility of jail.

My own experience as a public defender supported my belief that some people deserved life sentences. My clients have included a seventy-year-old man who raped his own five-year-old grandson, and a drunk driver who crushed a little boy between two parked cars—then stood unmoved during the heart-wrenching victim impact statement given by the boy's father, who witnessed the killing but was helpless to stop it. One client chilled me to my core: as a juvenile, he had graduated from burglary and auto theft to armed robbery, holding up three separate victims in the course of two days. The first victim was a young mother playing with her kids in a park; the second was an eleven-year-old on a bike. My client preyed on the vulnerable. When he took their property at gunpoint, he said the same thing: "*I want that.*" It was the object he cared about; the people meant nothing to him.

I recognized David Biro in him. I had forgiven David, said his name, even prayed for him. But I still wasn't certain I wanted him to serve less than his full life sentence.

Back to that conversation with Mark Osler: we were talking, lawyer to lawyer, about the U.S. Supreme Court ruling in the *Miller* case striking down one of the sentences David was serving—mandatory juvenile life without parole. *Miller* held that judges could no longer impose a mandatory sentence of life without parole on juveniles; judges would have to take a host of factors into consideration, including the age of the offender at the time of the crime, before a life sentence could be given.

David was serving a mandatory life sentence for killing Nancy and Richard. He was serving a discretionary life sentence for intentionally killing their unborn child. That meant I could expect that David would seek a resentencing hearing to reduce at least part of his sentence to less than life, based on the *Miller* decision.

I had no idea whether I could support the release of David Biro at such a hearing. "He's still remorseless," I told Osler.

"How do you know that?" he responded, leaning across the table. "You don't know that. You've never even spoken to him."

I was stunned. He was right.

I had spoken about the murders and forgiveness all over the world: France, Ireland, Mongolia, Japan, and all across the United States. I had written about forgiving David Biro, given speeches at churches and schools and conferences. The one person I hadn't told: him. Never once had I communicated my forgiveness to David Biro.

I had waited all these years for him to apologize to me. I saw it now with startling clarity: I had to apologize to him, for never telling him that I had forgiven him. I had to go first.

That wasn't all. The Holy Spirit, the spirit of God that moves like wind, blowing things open, scattering debris, wasn't done with me yet.

On a Sunday morning, months later, I went to a "church on the beach" service held by Christ Church, a charming, ivy-covered stone church set on a hill near Lake Michigan in the town where I live. It's a pleasant change from the Gothic formality of my Presbyterian church in downtown Chicago. You spread out a blanket on the grass on a bluff overlooking the beach, kick off your flip-flops, bring your dog to loll beside you. I arrived late, just in time to hear the priest, a man in a black shirt and white collar, cargo shorts and Birkenstocks, begin his homily.

He was talking about how the Sunday after the Episcopal church's national convention is like its own liturgical season: the season of complaints. Every year, he said, on the Sunday after the convention he feels like a human dartboard. Members of his congregation call or e-mail him, demanding to know: Why did the church vote in favor of *that*? How could the church decide *this*?

The priest's response: When you get a thousand Episcopalians in a room, you get a thousand different opinions. "It's a mess!" the priest observed, half-ruefully, half-cheerfully. He threw up his hands. "A mess!"

He went on, tying the messiness of the human condition to stories from Scripture. One was about King David, taking a woman who was the wife of another man, then arranging that man's death in battle. Another was the awful story of the beheading of John the Baptist because of Herod's moment of misbegotten pride.

"We are a mess, all of us. And how does God respond to that messiness? Mercy . . . mercy . . . *mercy*," the priest concluded, pausing between each word, his voice dropping to a whisper with the last.

That word hung in the still, sunlit air. We sat silent, no sound but the distant crash of waves on the beach, the song of birds overhead. The word lodged in my heart. *Mercy.*

We, the congregation, said that word a short time later, just before we lined up under the shade of a spreading tree to take the bread and wine. "Lamb of

God, you take away the sins of the world: have mercy upon us."

You take away the sins of the world, I pondered. *What does that mean?* Whatever it meant, I knew that it couldn't mean saying to any human being: We are taking the sin you committed and freezing it in time forever. No matter what you do, how much you repent and show remorse, you are forever only one thing— killer—and we will punish you endlessly for it.

I knew this in my heart: I could no longer support this merciless sentence of life without parole for juveniles.

And in the very next moment, like daylight breaking into darkness, I knew something else. I'd always thought that the only thing big enough to pay for the life of my sister was a life sentence for her killer. Now I understood: the only thing big enough to equal the loss of her life was for him to be found.

Chapter 9

THE LETTER

LATE AT NIGHT ON THE LAST DAY OF SEPTEMBER 2012, I put my two sons to bed and crept downstairs in the darkened house. I sat at the computer, turned on a small desk light, and typed this letter:

I scarcely know how to write this, how to begin. I have given it much thought.

You know who I am: one of the sisters of Nancy Bishop Langert.

I know who you are: the son of Nick and Joan Biro, who knew my parents, and the person convicted of killing Nancy, her husband and their baby.

We saw each other every day during your trial at 26th and California. Since then, we have talked about each other, but never to each other.

I have heard news of you: how prison has been hard at times because of your association with me and my sisters. I am sorry for that. Nancy above all was about love; she never would have wanted her death to result in more brutality, even to the person who took her life.

You have heard news of me: how I have forgiven you for killing my family members. I never conveyed that forgiveness to you directly; I am sorry for that, too. It was wrong to tell other people and not the most important person of all: you.

When, a few years ago, a campaign began to abolish the sentence you are serving—juvenile life without parole—I resisted that effort. I lobbied the Illinois legislature, successfully, to stop the bill that would have changed the law to prohibit the sentence. I became a public voice for keeping you and others serving that sentence locked up forever. I am sorry for that now, too.

I am writing to tell you that, and to explain why. You deserve to know.

It's a story that begins with a law professor whose life's work has been about mercy. An ex-prosecutor, he has spent his career arguing against harsh sentences such as the death penalty and juvenile life without parole. He gave me a book about forgiveness with an article by his former colleague, pastor and academic Dr. Randall O'Brien. Randall wrote in the article that each of us has an obligation to reconcile with those who have wronged us.

That floored me. Until that moment, I thought that forgiveness was enough. That I could simply say, in essence, I forgive you, and now I am shaking you like dust off my feet. I never saw reconciliation as possible because you have never taken responsibility for killing my family members.

How do I reconcile with someone whose position is, I have not wronged you?

I called Randall to ask him that question. He responded with some stunning observations.

First, that you and I are no different in the eyes of God. I am someone who has fallen short and hurt God's heart; I have sinned, to use that Biblical word, just as you have. You are a child of God, created in God's image, just as I am. God loves you every bit as much as me; nothing you have done could ever stop God from loving you. The division I have made between us—you, guilty murderer, me, innocent victims' family member—was a false divide. I was wrong to do that.

Randall's second observation was this: How did Jesus respond to the people who were taking his life, in the very moment they were killing him? He prayed for them: Father, forgive them; they don't know what they are doing.

It struck me that I had never prayed for you. I had never even said your name. That was wrong of me, too. So I did pray for you, in the garden outside Kenilworth Union Church—you know the place—where Nancy and Richard and their baby are buried, alongside my father, who found their bodies the morning after they died.

Here is what I have come to believe: sentences like the death penalty and life without parole reflect our need to find a response to something as heinous as the murder of innocents equal in weight and gravity to the crime itself.

The only thing that could possibly pay for the loss of Nancy, her husband and their baby is this nearly-impossible thing: that you would make your way home to God, the way the Prodigal Son in one of Jesus' parables finds his way home.

So I can no longer support the sentence of juvenile life without parole. It says to you, and to every other person serving that sentence: never. No matter what you do, how you may be transformed, or who you become, we will never even give you a chance to get out of prison.

That means I will argue in the upcoming session of the Illinois General Assembly to change the law, so that there will be a possibility of parole at some point in cases like yours. I owe it to you to say it to you first, before I say it publicly. That doesn't mean that I will advocate for you to get out of prison, only that there should be that possibility in the future.

This will be difficult for me, and create tension with people I love. Part of my own pain has been that you have never expressed remorse for the deaths you caused. I want that to change. I hope it will.

I invite you to talk with me. If you want that, let me know and I will come to see you.

With that, I stopped typing, printed out the letter, and signed my name at the bottom.

The next day was a crisp Monday morning. I walked to the post office, the main one in the Village of Winnetka, a few blocks from my home. In my hand was a large manila envelope containing the letter I had written the night before. I pulled down the handle to one of the large blue mailboxes out front and was about to drop in the envelope. It was addressed to David Biro, Pontiac Correctional Center, Pontiac, Illinois.

Something stopped me short—an image that flashed through my mind of a small child's hand pulling down that same handle on the big blue mailbox: David Biro's. He had been a boy here, in Winnetka. He might have come here, perhaps on an errand with his mother, and put some mail in that same box. Perhaps the Christmas cards my family had received from his, bearing photos of David when he was just a child, had been mailed here.

I held the envelope poised in the air for a moment and breathed a prayer, asking the Holy Spirit to do its work. I dropped the letter in.

How would he respond? Would he respond at all? I had visions of him reading my letter and laughing—showing it to a cell mate, maybe, scoffing at my earnest foolishness. He might crumple it up and toss it into a prison receptacle. He might write back, angrily telling me where I could shove my letter and my lofty words about God.

I had no idea. All I knew was this: it was out of my hands now. It was in the hands of God.

Weeks went by and I heard nothing from Biro. I imagined that he might have sent the letter to a lawyer, to get advice about whether to respond, and if so, how. A cautious attorney might counsel him to say nothing at all. I began to think I would never hear back.

Then one day, when I was coming back from court, I stopped at the mailbox in the public defender's office where I work and pulled a stack of mail from the slot: some returned subpoenas, some junk mail, and a large manila envelope with a return address from a downstate prison. I thought nothing of that last piece of mail; clients often write me from prison. I took the pile of mail to my desk and tossed it there, to look at later.

But something peeked out at me from the upper left corner of the large manila envelope: the return address didn't just say "Pontiac." Above that address, in small, neat print, was the name Biro.

My heart leapt. I looked closer, to be sure I wasn't dreaming. It was from him, David Biro. I picked up the envelope; it had weight, it was thick. Whatever was inside, it was more than the one page my letter had been.

Needing quiet, I closed the door to my office and returned to my desk. I sat down and picked up the envelope, holding it my hands. I willed them to open it, but they refused to budge. I could not do it.

What if I opened it, and the letter was a screed of derision and defiance? Or worse, an attempt at manipulation, filled with lies? I put down the envelope, intact.

It sat there, untouched, for the rest of the workday. At the end of the day, I gathered up my belongings: purse, coat. I glanced at the envelope on my desk and realized I could not leave such an irreplaceable object unattended all night. I picked it up and took it home.

There it stayed, sitting on my dresser. Each time I thought I had summoned the courage to slit open the end of the envelope and pull out its contents, something inside me shrank from the task. I could not do this alone.

I called a friend and made an unusual request: would he open and read the letter first? He readily answered yes. Two days after I received the letter, he did.

I am drawing a circle around that moment; it is a memory so precious to me that I want to keep close its details. Here is what I can tell: He took the envelope from my hands and sent me on an errand—made up, I realized later, so that, as he read, I would not see the expression on his face, and wonder and worry. The generosity and thoughtfulness of that will stay with me forever.

I returned almost an hour later carrying a plastic bag with the items he'd sent me to get. He was seated outdoors; it was nearly evening. The late afternoon light bathed his face. I looked at him searchingly. He was holding a fistful of lined notebook paper covered with small, neat writing in pencil. He looked up at my anxious face and smiled, a calm, quiet smile. "It's good," he said.

I let go the breath I had been holding in. He had been kind enough to answer right away the question looming in my heart: *How is it?* My heart lightened with relief.

I dropped down into the seat next to him. "I'll read it to you," he said. He told me later that he wanted me to hear the words of my sister's killer spoken in a voice I knew and trusted.

I sat still, drinking it in. Biro's letter to me began like this:

Dear Jeanne,

Hello there. As I write to you, I hope that you and your family are all doing well. Thank you for writing to me. I appreciated your letter very much and in many ways it touched me very deeply. I commend you on your courage in writing. I know it must have been difficult to write to me and put yourself out there, especially as you had no idea how I was going to respond. I think by the end of this letter, you'll understand better what I mean when I say that it took courage to write.

One thing I liked about your letter was that it had a kind of tone to it, that I interpreted as saying "Let's cut the crap

*and be honest with each other." I agree. I don't want to keep
you in suspense any longer, so let me get right to the point.*

*I know that for a long time you and your family have
been looking for me to confess to the murders I committed
years ago. Of course, as you know in the past, I have always
maintained my "innocence." Well, for a lot of reasons which
I'll get into in a little bit, I think the time has come for me
to drop the charade and finally be honest. You're right, I am
guilty of killing your sister Nancy, and her husband Richard.
I also want to take this opportunity to express my deepest con-
dolences and apologize to you.*

A cry escaped my lips, a kind of sob buried so deep,
I hadn't known it was there. I leaned forward, fingers
pressed to my mouth. To hear those words: *You're right,
I am guilty. . . .* I never thought I would hear that, ever. It
was more than I'd ever dreamed. My reader was right:
it was good.

I sat up and breathed deeply. He read on, for fifteen
pages, passages like these:

*You may wonder why I've finally decided to tell you the
truth. Well, let me see if I can explain a few things. . . .*

*I'm in prison, and this is a place where one is naturally
given to introspection and reflection. I can't even tell you the
number of hours I have spent contemplating my life, thinking
about the mistakes I've made or what might have been, and
I feel a great deal of regret over some of the things I've done.
Obviously I don't like having to live in prison and miss out on
so much of life (who would?) but I can honestly say that in
many respects this experience has been good for me.*

*. . . Over the years, I've done my best not to waste my
time in here and educate myself, and I've read a great number*

of books on a variety of different subjects including history, philosophy, religion, etc. . . . I'm not saying that I've become a moral person simply because I've read a lot of books. But I do think the process of educating myself has helped me to grow and mature as a person, and that in turn has led to me doing a lot of critical thinking and reflection about my situation.

Biro discussed watching television news stories about heinous murders and feeling sympathy for the victims and revulsion toward the killers:

When I see different crimes being discussed on t.v., it reminds me of my own crime and I feel the sting of shame and embarrassment even more. These days, not a day goes by when I don't think about the crime I committed. Every day I wish I could take it back, not only because I dislike life in prison, but also because I wish I could give you back the lives of your loved ones.

. . . I don't know how much my apology means to you at this point. It might be "a day late and a dollar short" as the old saying goes. But this is all I have to give. If I could give you back the lives of Nancy and Richard, I would.

Explaining why he had waited so long to take responsibility, Biro wrote something that struck me as courageous:

I only held back . . . because of my reluctance to give a full confession which I know from this point on I can never retract. That's exactly what this is. I'm sure you realize that from this point on I can never again say I'm innocent. You have my handwritten confession right here.

It was true. He had given me something he could never take back: an admission to the murders in his own hand.

Biro came to a close by agreeing to meet with me, telling me how to get on his visitors list, and suggesting that I call his father about visiting procedures and directions to the prison. The letter ended:

I'm sorry to take so long responding to your letter, but as you can see, I had a lot to say, and I rewrote this letter a couple of times because I wanted to make sure I said everything the right way. As I reread this letter, I still feel as if I didn't express myself as well as I would have liked to. I wish my words were more eloquent and my thoughts flowed better. But alas, I think we both accept that I'm not William Shakespeare. And if my words fell short in their beauty, please know that they were sincere.

Sincerely,

David Biro

I sat in stunned silence, letting the words sink in. My mind filled with wonder. Who could have imagined this? Not in my wildest dreams did I suppose David Biro might do what he had resisted doing ever since the murders: confess and say he was sorry. It was beyond anything I could have asked for—and I knew, even as I heard his apology, that it would not have come if I had not gone first. The time I spent waiting for that apology! That was the price I paid for my coldness toward Biro, for holding myself aloof.

Eager to follow up on the offer of a visit, I acted right away, sending the prison the required information so I could get in to see him. I wanted to act on David's suggestion that I call his father as well. I had not spoken to Nick Biro since the night his son was arrested, more than two decades earlier. My response to the grief-stricken father had been curt. I knew what I had to do: apologize to him, too.

I hesitated, a little afraid. I had been a voice for keeping his son in prison all these years. How would he react to a phone call from me, out of nowhere?

One February morning, I was leaving the gym after an early morning workout. I ascended the stairs and walked into a world radiant with sunlight. It wasn't the usual thin, pale light of Chicago in winter; the sky was sapphire blue. The air was gentle and still. The distant, sweet sound of birds chirping echoed from the trees all around. I sat down on the curb of the parking lot and turned my face upward to the sun, soaking in its warmth. I crossed my arms over my knees and rested, flooded with peace. *Now*, I thought. I pulled out my cell phone and called Mr. Biro.

An answering machine picked up, with the voice of Nick Biro just as I remembered it, slow paced, kindly sounding. I left a message saying how sorry I was for our last phone call, and that I had written to David and hoped to visit him. Would Nick call me back? I gave my number and said I hoped we could speak soon.

I hung up and breathed another prayer, like the one I'd said silently when I dropped my letter to David in the mailbox. *Holy Spirit of God, do something with this.*

Nick Biro called back the next day. He was grace itself, saying that he couldn't imagine what I had to apologize for, that he was the one who was sorry, for my family's tragedy. We agreed to get together on the upcoming Saturday.

We met at a local coffee shop with big windows the sun shone through, wooden tables, and a cozy fireplace.

We sat on a small couch in front of that fireplace and talked for two hours.

He looked the same as he had when I knew him through my parents—tall, with a broad, congenial face—but his hair had whitened, and his hearing had diminished. He wore dark pants and a thick green sweater. He had the same courtly, old-school manners my father had had. Speaking to him reminded me of my dad and made me miss him acutely.

The story of Nick Biro's last two decades emerged: he had gone to prison to visit his son once every two weeks, without fail, ever since David was sentenced. Mr. Biro was relieved that he had just passed the test to renew his driver's license; he always drove, alone, to visit David. Even though David had a brother and sister, Mr. Biro was David's only regular visitor. He was eighty-two years old.

Those visits could be arduous. When David was in Menard prison, in a far-flung part of Illinois, Mr. Biro would travel around two hundred miles, sometimes only to find that the prison was locked down because of a riot or a fight. He would have no choice but to turn around and go home. When David was in Stateville, a notoriously tough prison nearer Chicago, the guards could be difficult. Pontiac, where David was incarcerated now, was a better place, Mr. Biro said, closer to Chicago. The staff was more pleasant, but very strict about rules for visitors. One day, he had left the window of his car partly rolled down. He was called out and told that was not allowed; he had to roll it up.

Mr. Biro said all this not as a complaint, but as a word of caution. He gave me a list of rules: When I went to see David, I should call first, to see if visits were still on. I should check to be sure nothing illegal was in my car. I could not bring in a cell phone. As he ticked down the list, he pulled out a sheet of paper: it was his written driving directions to Pontiac, down to landmarks such as the McDonald's restaurant where he would stop for coffee before heading to the prison.

Then he told me about the lockers inside the guardhouse, where visitors must lock their car keys and any other belongings while they are visiting. You drop two quarters in a slot and pull out a key. "I brought quarters for you," he said, pressing them into my palm. Then he took both my hands in his, looked me in the eyes, and said, "God bless you."

It felt just like that: a blessing from God.

I walked out, marveling. I understood for the first time what Jesus was saying to us about apologies: you go first. Don't wait. Seeing the fruits that my apologies had borne, I asked myself: why didn't I do this sooner? Wasn't that what Nancy was telling me all along, with her message of love?

Chapter 10

THE VISIT

THE DRIVE TO PONTIAC PRISON FROM MY HOME IS 113 miles down I-55, a flat highway stretching through cornfields and small towns. You pass a few more prison sites: Joliet, Morris, Dwight. The landscape is dotted with signs touting antique stores, pickup trucks, places to eat. Silos and farmhouses line the sides of the road. There is a wind farm on the left—dozens of tall, white windmills with three blades turning gracefully clockwise—and a small cemetery nestled under pine trees on the right. Turn on the radio, and you will find more than one station talking about Jesus.

It was early on a Sunday morning, March 3, 2013, and I was heading to Pontiac to see David Biro for the first time.

Downstate Illinois was an oddly familiar place to be traveling through on the way to this unfamiliar destination. My parents' families on both sides had come from there.

My father grew up in Pekin, Illinois. He came from a farm family; his father, Wilbur Lee Bishop, worked at the Caterpillar plant for four decades before he retired. A modest man who wore cardigan sweaters with two pockets—one for his pipe, and the other for his tobacco pouch—my grandfather Bishop had risen from pushing a broom to being a highly respected engineer at the plant. He challenged his son to do better than he had. One day when my father was young, Wilbur took him out to a tennis court and beat him in a game. Stung, my father vowed never to let that happen again. He hit ball after ball against the brick wall of the local junior high school. He ended up making the Junior Davis Cup tennis team and earned a spot on the University of Illinois tennis team on an athletic scholarship. He was the first of his family to go to college.

It was at the U of I where my father met my mother, a townie who had grown up on East Daniel Street in Champaign, Illinois. Her father, John J. Bresee, was an engineer, architect, artist, and lawyer. Mostly, though, he was a prosecutor, elected to multiple terms as the state's attorney of Champaign County. A Republican, he was the county's chief prosecutor from 1942 to 1956; he was later reelected and served during the turbulent period between 1964 and 1968. He tried cases himself, including murders (my mother could recount verbatim parts of his closing argument in a notorious ice-pick killing, about the "hand of fate" that pointed to the defendant). I thought of him when I became a public defender. I was proud of his service; I know he would have been proud of mine.

Much of my childhood was spent driving south from Chicago to visit my relatives, in places that seemed strange and exotic compared to the big, sleek, and silver city from which I had come. When I was little, we went at Christmas and Easter. On Thanksgivings, my whole extended family of aunts and uncles, cousins and second cousins, gathered at my Great-aunt Ruth's farm in Rossville, Illinois. A long dirt driveway to the big white house led past a pasture, where two small ponies grazed. There were apple trees you could climb and hay bales in the barn you could jump on. Peacocks roamed the place, scattering shimmering feathers that Aunt Ruth gathered in vases all over her house, glorious bouquets of purple and blue. We would assemble around tables laden with turkey, mashed potatoes, and pie, and sing the doxology, which always made my grandfather Bresee cry. As the final Amen was sung, you could hear the shuddering of his suppressed sobs and see tears streaming down his face. After dinner, the men would smoke and play cards, while the women cleared the dishes and washed them in the kitchen, singing along to the radio.

Those memories spun in my head as I drove to Pontiac. My mind was racing, anticipating the visit ahead. Too deep in thought to turn on the radio, I drove in silence but for the hum of tires on the road. The sun was just coming up, spreading gold over fields that flitted by on either side, bare cornstalks sticking out of the snow.

What would I say to David Biro when I got there? I had no plan for this meeting, no script. I didn't know what words to speak when we met. Both hands nervously gripping the wheel of my car, I tried to think of something, to conjure the words out of my own wisdom. I kept fumbling, failing. At last it struck me: I needed to get out of the way and ask God to do the talking. I started to pray: *God, let me listen for your voice. Let me say what you want to say. Open my heart. Open his.*

After two hours on the road, I spotted the exit sign that David Biro's father had told me to look for, Pontiac Flanagan. I turned off and followed the exit around, heading toward the town and the prison. I passed a Super 8 Motel, a Walmart, an Arby's restaurant. Right before the railroad tracks, there was the McDonald's, just as Nick Biro had told me. Almost there! Scanning the driving instructions Mr. Biro had given me, I drove over the tracks and turned right a few blocks later.

The prison loomed straight ahead, a short distance away. I was shocked at how close it was to the small houses in this modest residential neighborhood; there were homes literally across the street from the prison gates. What must it be like, I wondered, to live in one of those houses, to take out your trash or wash your car or mow your lawn and see always in the corner of your eye this warehouse for human beings?

As I pulled into the prison parking lot, gravel crunched under my tires.

∽

"I'm Jeanne Bishop," I said, a nervous few minutes later, taking the hand of the prisoner who walked toward me.

The man before me bore only a passing resemblance to the teenager I had seen walk out of court years before. The bushy brown hair was gone, replaced by a prison buzz cut. Gone, too, was the cocky expression; the person who stepped through the door looked nervous, eager. He was no longer a skinny high schooler; he stood at six foot five and had added a stone of weight. His arms were covered with tattoos.

I took it all in—the crinkles at the corners of his eyes, his receding hairline, the way his baggy prison clothes seemed to sag on his frame. His face was shiny from the stiflingly close prison air; his hand was warm when I took it to shake. He had loomed larger than life in my mind, and now, here he was in the flesh, startlingly human. *This is not a monster,* I thought. *This is a man.*

How foolish, the way I had mythologized him! In the years since Nancy's murder, I had turned him into this fiend, a savage too frightening to ever let out of prison. He was the person who, when my children were born, I feared would somehow come lurking in the night and try to hurt them. How had I ever given him such sway over my imagination? I saw in these surroundings how powerless he was. He was caught, as helpless as an animal in a trap.

He told me the number of the cubicle where I was to go for the visit, then went back through the door with the guard. I walked the opposite way to a long, narrow room lined with cubicles, two chairs at each one. I sat at a small white desk topped with a pane of thick glass. A moment later, David sat down on the opposite side of that glass. He smiled again, eyes looking expectantly into mine.

"Thank you for seeing me," I began, pulling my chair closer to the glass. We were speaking into small microphones on either side. (Later those would be replaced by telephones.) I told him I had met with his dad, and how thoughtful he had been, giving me quarters and directions. David asked how my trip had been; I asked what Pontiac was like. It was a kind of throat-clearing, to put each other at ease. Neither of us talked about the murders at the outset.

I didn't want to. As soon as I sat down, I knew what I wanted: to get to know him, to understand the arc that led from the little boy I'd seen on a Christmas card to someone who could take a .357 Magnum, put it to the back of a grown man's head, and pull the trigger.

I tried to go there, to get him to trace that trajectory, but I soon grasped that he wanted—he *needed*—to tell me about the night itself: Saturday, April 7, 1990. He had to talk about it, to tell me his story.

He spoke in a warm voice and seemed eager to tell his story. I am recounting our conversation as I remember it; because visitors are not allowed to bring anything into the prison, I could not take down our words verbatim. I quote David only where I remember exactly what he said.

He said he'd been a kid who had always felt poor in a town of very rich people. He didn't have the kind of money his friends at New Trier came from. His family didn't have the same cars or clothes or take the same vacations as the people around him. So he started to commit burglaries.

Why did you get a gun? I broke in. My clients never bring a gun to do a burglary.

David said he'd always been fascinated with guns, since he was a little kid. He and other boys would take BB guns into the woods near Crow Island School, where I went to elementary school as a child, and shoot at animals. Later, he forged the paperwork needed to buy a firearm because he wanted more than just a BB gun; he wanted a real gun.

If you wanted money and you had a gun, why not just do armed robberies on the street? Why break into people's homes? I asked.

David said he would need some kind of accomplice or getaway vehicle for that. The burglaries were something he could do alone, undetected.

Drawing again on my experience as a public defender, I said, My burglary clients never want to encounter people in the homes they break into. They get in and get out. You waited. Why?

He said that his plan the night of the murders was to wait for the homeowners—Nancy and Richard—to return so he could take their wallets and car.

But that makes no sense, I countered. How could you take their car keys and wallets without them seeing you? You'd have to go in knowing you were going to kill them. Once they were found dead, having their car would link you to their murder.

This is the way a naive sixteen-year-old kid from Winnetka thinks, David answered. It was completely stupid and unrealistic. A lot of the guys here in prison with me grew up with criminals—an older brother or an uncle—who could teach them how to commit crimes. I didn't. A mentor in crime would have told me, for instance, that you never, ever keep the gun. You get rid of it. I kept it, he said.

Why? I asked.

In case I wanted to use it again, David responded.

Why did you pick that townhouse? I wanted to know. It was a question my mother particularly had wanted me to ask when she heard I was going to visit David Biro.

David explained that he was familiar with the row of townhouses where Nancy and Richard lived. It was the ideal place to exit quickly, by descending the steep hill behind the townhouses sloping down to the commuter train tracks and the path that stretched alongside. The hill and trail would be dark and deserted at that time of night; he could run down the hill and slip away. David had rung the doorbells of each of the townhouses to see who was home; then he tested the back gates to see which were locked. He wanted an unlocked gate so he could escape through the back yard. Nancy and Richard's townhouse fit the bill perfectly. No one was home; their back gate was unlocked.

That is all it took to seal their fate, I thought, aghast. *Those small details marked them for death.*

David went on with his story. He used the glass cutter to enter through their sliding glass door in the back, for exactly the reason I'd surmised: so that neighbors wouldn't hear the sound of breaking glass. He came in and looked around the place for about an hour, looking for something to steal. Then he waited for Nancy and Richard to come home. When he heard them walking in, David said, he suddenly had second thoughts about going through with his plan. He started to try to dash out the side door, but it was locked from the inside.

That is true, I realized. You have to unlock that door with a key from the inside to get out. That is a detail he couldn't have made up.

Now David was face to face with Nancy and Richard. Richard demanded to know what he was doing there. David displayed the gun.

I thought the story would be familiar at this point: Nancy pleads for their lives, tries to negotiate, offers him the money from her paycheck. But that wasn't the story David told. What he said next stunned me: it was Richard, the strong, silent one, and not Nancy, the chatty one, who did most of the talking. It was Richard who told Biro that Nancy was pregnant ("My wife is expecting; please don't hurt her"), who kept proposing ways that David could leave them unharmed and still get away. Richard never stopped trying to suggest a way out, a way the lives of his wife and child could be spared, right up to the moment the gun was to his head.

I uttered a soft cry. To know what a hero my brother-in-law was in his last moments, how much he loved and tried to protect Nancy, how valiantly he strove to save her—that was a gift I never expected. I should have guessed it—but I never would have known without David Biro.

David went on. After the gun went off accidentally when he was spooked by the dog, he told Nancy and Rich to go to the basement, that he would lock them in and leave.

Why didn't you do what you said? Why not lock them in and go? I demanded.

I just wanted to finish it, David replied.

Finish it. The words stabbed at my heart. That *it* he had wanted to finish was my sister and her husband and their baby. Why did you kill Richard the way you did? I asked. It looked like an assassination, an execution.

When he was young and aiming his gun at birds and squirrels in Crow Island Woods, David explained, one friend told him: Shoot them in the head, so they can't run away.

Then why did you shoot Nancy where you did, in her pregnant belly? I went on, my throat tight.

Nancy had seen what happened to Rich and had huddled in a corner of the basement in the dark, covering her head. David told me he had fired twice into her body, then run out in panic.

The whole next day, Palm Sunday, he had walked around the town in a cold sweat, looking over his shoulder, expecting to be arrested. Why? Because he didn't know if Nancy was dead or alive. He knew he had killed Rich instantly; Nancy was still living when David had fled. Neighbors might have heard the gunshots and called police. The police could have asked Nancy to describe her assailant. If she had described a skinny, brown-haired teenager, the police could have shown her one of David's mug shots or his picture in a New Trier yearbook. She could have looked at the photo and said, "That's him."

When David heard the news that night that a young couple had been found murdered in their home, he was relieved. He was thankful that he had succeeded in killing Nancy, too. Again, that had the ring of truth to it. I believed that part of the story. It hurt, but I believed it.

I was struck by his courage in being so open with me, in telling me details, even when they put him in a bad light. "I don't want you to hate me," he said at one point. Those words startled me; they were the mirror image of what I had said in the Winnetka police station the day I learned that Nancy and Richard and their baby had been murdered: "I don't want to hate anyone." I still didn't.

I was taken, too, with David's sensitivity to how I might feel in response to what he was telling me. "Are you sure you want to hear this?" he would ask, before a particularly difficult revelation. It was a long way from the brash young man who, when he was first arrested, stuck out his tongue at press photographers who snapped his picture in the back of a police car. I always said yes, I did want to hear it. I wanted to hear all of it. I was grateful to fill in the gaps in my knowledge about what happened to my family members, to learn new things, such as Richard's extraordinary heroism.

David asked me questions, too. We spent time clearing up our mutual misconceptions, the way you fish dead leaves out of a pool to make the water clear. People who said they were journalists or activists had come to visit him on and off, over the years, but he was always suspicious. Had my family sent them, to spy on him? I don't want you to take this the wrong way, I replied, but we didn't give you a second thought. We didn't want to think about you. So, no, we didn't send people in undercover to check on you.

I told David about the damage he had done to my mother, whose youngest daughter and son-in-law and first grandchild were ripped from her in one senseless act. How at first, she had been in a trancelike state of grief, and then in fully realized agony. She would wait till she was alone in the house, then wander around looking at pictures of Nancy, in so much pain that she could not even cry; instead, she would keen, doubling over and making a noise that sounded to her own ears like the moaning of an animal. A dark shadow passed across his face as I spoke. He looked thoughtful, subdued, as if the pain he had caused my mother had never occurred to him before. I thought: *This is the best victim impact statement I could ever ask for. He is face to face with me, listening and taking it in. He* has *to hear me.*

One such story was enough, on this visit; I wanted to let it sink in. Later, on other visits, I would pick other stories to tell David. How my father had to find the bodies of his daughter and son-in-law, lying frozen in pools of blood, and the grim pall that had cast over the last years of his life. How my boys had grown up without the aunt and uncle and cousin they should have known. ("Mommy, I wish I had that baby cousin," my younger son had said to me on his first visit to their grave.) The anguish that David's confession to one classmate and false accusation of another had caused them and their families.

I wanted David to see that Nancy and Richard were not his only victims; killing them was like dropping a pebble into a pond and sending out ripples of evil. He had hurt the police and evidence technicians who had to witness the carnage he had left at the townhouse. He had hurt his parents and brother and sister by putting them through the ordeal of his arrest, trial, sentencing, and imprisonment. He had hurt every person who ever knew and loved Nancy and Rich—friends, coworkers, classmates, neighbors, relatives. He had robbed every person to whom Nancy and Richard and their child ever would have done good. David had an obligation now, I told him, to send out ripples of goodness instead, to be that force for good wherever he was, in prison or out.

Was he getting any of this? It was hard to tell. I heard some troubling things from him during that first visit. Some self-centeredness: he saw himself as the victim of biased media and bad lawyering. That had a familiar ring; I had heard the same complaint countless times over the years from clients I had represented, people who wanted to spread the blame for their predicament. Superiority: David expressed a sense of being better than some of the inmates around him.

And yet, I sensed that his remorse was real. He looked genuinely stricken when he spoke of wishing he could bring Nancy and Richard back, take back what he did that night. He never once mentioned the legal status of his case, never referred to the change in the law that could lead to his release. He never asked me to take his side if he were resentenced someday. What he seemed to want, above all else, was some sort of understanding—for me to know who he was—and for some kind of connection, for us to have a relationship, human to human.

That connection would be costly. I knew going in that the visit would not be a made-for-TV moment; we

would not instantly throw our arms around each other
and begin to cry. We would start slowly, cautiously, like
a toddler gingerly pulling itself up to its feet, testing
how much weight its wobbling legs could bear.

What we had to say to one another was hard. The
wounds were deep, on both sides. He had taken my
sister; I had helped take his freedom. We were both
aggrieved, wanting the other person to understand. The
stories we had to tell, and hear, were complicated. It
would take time, untangling those stories, like patiently
trying to pull apart the chains of two necklaces knotted
together.

These were the first fumbling birth pangs of reconciliation. Our reconciliation was not pretty, or perfect.
Nor did I expect it to be. I expected it to be as messy as
the two of us were.

("And how does God respond to that messiness?" I
could hear the priest on the beach saying. "Mercy . . .
mercy . . . mercy.")

I walked out of Pontiac prison that day thinking, *I
don't know how this will turn out. But I do know it is right.*
My friend Susan Stabile wrote to me once: "That is the
point with God: we don't get all the *i*'s dotted and the
t's crossed in advance. We're asked to say yes, knowing
the path ahead is clouded in uncertainty—to say yes in
faith that God will be with us no matter what."

I had taken the first step without knowing what was
ahead. It was unfamiliar terrain, like the paths in the
hills of Scotland on the trip Nancy and Richard and
I took—so different from my territory, Illinois, where
streets and roadways are even and straight. There, it's
said you can sit on your front porch and watch your

dog run away for a week. Scotland was a place of rises and curves; even if you were headed the right way, you couldn't be sure, because the streets turned and bowed.

I was entering a new place now, a new journey, more like Scotland than Illinois. Finally, finally, I was ready to walk those ancient and uneven streets of forgiveness and wonder.

Chapter 11

THE COST

THERE IS A MOMENT, A SPLIT-SECOND BEFORE YOU EMBARK into the unknown: when your parent lets go of the back of your bicycle, training wheels removed, launching you to pedal on your own, or when you hover for the first time on the edge of a diving board, staring down at the great chasm of air and water looming below. You pedal, you leap, and in that instant it is exhilarating. Sometimes you plunge in and rise to the top of that water, buoyant and bubbling with excitement. Other times, you fall hard, and feel the pain your daring cost you. Often, you feel both.

Visiting David Biro exacted such a cost. Family and friends who continued to support the sentence I no longer believed in—juvenile life without parole—were appalled at my choice. They felt betrayed. There were difficult backyard conversations, phone calls, e-mails, many so personal and private that I cannot write about them here. A Christian friend observed that he now understood what Jesus meant in Matthew 10:35, "For I have come to set . . . a daughter against her mother." The divisions were that close to the bone. My mother and I, thank God, were and are still close—but I know I hurt others who grappled with what I had done.

I wrote a piece for CNN's Belief Blog about praying for David Biro and my change of heart about juvenile life sentences. The post generated almost two thousand comments from readers responding to the piece. I didn't read them—I usually never do. My friend Steve Drizin, a lawyer and advocate for juveniles, got in touch after the piece appeared to see if I was okay. Sounding concerned, he asked how I was coping with the viciousness of most of those comments. I didn't know what he meant. A long while later, I took a look:

- "Your sister's murderer went to the wrong house. He should have went to yours."
- "Anyone who would give that pos [piece of shit] another chance to do that to another family/ baby is mentally unbalanced. What you need is a good shrink."
- "Jeanne, please stay OUT of the criminal justice system: Do not further pollute it!"
- "Repulsive. If believing in this mythical ghost named 'Jesus' makes one work for the release

of the cold-blooded killer of your family, then someone needs to slap reason back into you."

- "If I was living in your state I would challenge your right to practice law, have you retested on the bar, and limit your practice to the ticket clinic, you my dear are a loser."

- "Your mind is diseased . . . your dead relatives who's graves you have now spit upon, are turning over in their graves at your cowardice and betrayal."

Other people described me as "cold and heartless," "unhealthy," "weak minded," "naïve," "sicko," "cruel," "troubled," "delusional," "gullible," "disgusting," and, my favorite, "pea head."

To call someone a pea head is to invite them back to the taunts and miseries of middle school. The truth, though, is that inside all of us, including me, is that gawky, insecure middle schooler. It was that remnant within that recoiled from these words, which were meant to push me away from them and society, a rejection of my truest self. That child within, an Oklahoma girl with long dark hair mowing the lawn in her bathing suit, crumpled.

Other notes hurt in a different way. An elderly couple whose daughter had been murdered wrote me a long letter full of pain and fury, quoting Scripture and calling me selfish and satanic. It covered nine pages, typewritten, single-spaced. The time and energy it must have taken!

A small, stubborn part of me rebelled at what I read in that letter; it felt wrong and unfair. As I read over the charges leveled at me, I saw clearly that I had two choices. I could write back refuting each point, defending myself, arguing the validity of my position, engaging in a potentially endless back-and-forth about who was right. Or I could see the letter for what it was, a howl of agony from two parents who dearly loved the child they lost. I had never lost a child; I could not begin to comprehend the abyss of their grief.

I wrote a short handwritten note on my personal stationery. I told them how sorry I was for the death of their child, how clear it was that they were still in great pain over that loss. I enclosed a check contributing to the foundation they had established in her memory and asked them to accept it. I prayed God's blessings on them.

They sent back a courteous handwritten note a short time afterward, thanking me for my letter and gift to their foundation. I treasured it. It felt like two hands clasping.

Later, one Saturday morning when I was speaking about forgiveness to the men's group at my church, the husband from the couple who had written that letter to me was in the audience. We shook each other's hands afterward; we talked about our common ground and where we diverged. It was calm and respectful and kind and full of grace; it felt like the kingdom of God.

I have learned so many lessons from this journey! One is that you can hear some Bible verses your whole life and not understand what they mean; then, suddenly, God gives you a moment of revelation. The light shines; the meaning is uncovered. *Aha! Now I get it.*

Take Jesus' admonition that we are to turn the other cheek—when our enemy strikes us on one cheek, we should turn and offer the other one (Matt. 5:39).

Before my epiphany, that baffled me. What did it mean? Are we really to say to the person who hits us, "Here, hit me again"? It seemed masochistic, nonsensical. The closest I could come to understanding it was the scene from the film *To Kill a Mockingbird* in which the defense lawyer Atticus Finch is set upon by the father of the alleged victim in a trial Atticus was defending. The furious father hurls abuse at Atticus and spits on him, spewing a gob of spittle onto Atticus's face. The lawyer doesn't strike back; with a withering glare, he wipes the spit off with a handkerchief and walks away. It is as if Atticus is saying, *You are beneath a response from me.* Now I realized that his act, though unexpected and gracious, was not quite the fulfillment of that Scripture.

The nine-page letter from the couple who lost their daughter taught me that Jesus was asking more than that. He wasn't asking merely that we refrain from striking back. He was asking us to say to the one who opposes us: I know you are angry and in pain. You think that hitting me will make you feel better. It won't—only God can heal that—but I am here. You can hit me as long as you want, till you get tired. I won't hit you back or flinch. Hit me on the left cheek; I will give you my right. When you are worn out by your rage, you will stop, and then we can talk.

I get it now: you absorb another's anger and respond with love.

One letter came that I couldn't respond to because it had no return address, just a name in the upper left corner. It was the name of the New Trier High School student who had turned in David Biro and testified against him at his trial.

I opened the letter, surprised. In one typed page, he wrote that he was "shocked and dismayed" to read that I supported the possibility—*the possibility*—that David Biro might be released from prison someday. He expressed fear for himself and his family. He noted that, years ago, he had made the decision to turn in David and had never regretted it. But, he concluded, *It should be obvious to everyone that I will certainly regret my decision if David is resentenced.*

I stood there with the letter in my hand, stunned. Though his fears were understandable, his words shocked me: *I will certainly regret my decision. . . .* He will regret bringing someone he knew to be a killer to justice? Regret ending, finally, the months-long agony of a family whose loved ones had been slaughtered? Regret thwarting the plan of the person he turned in to kill again? He would *regret* all that? I felt as if I had been mugged.

Other tensions were closer to home. It is one thing to be on the opposite side of strangers on an issue such as juvenile life sentences; it is quite another when the issue becomes a point of disagreement with family and friends. That's when your heart plays tug-of-war with itself. Agreeing to disagree is the solution, of course, and many people in my circle have been able to do it, on a host of issues: homosexuality and marriage equality, Republican vs. Democratic politics, the death penalty. Others have not been able to. It can be hard.

Just after I started visiting David Biro, I was asked to testify before an Illinois legislative committee in favor of a bill reforming juvenile life without parole sentences. The bill would give juveniles, including David, a chance to be resentenced and possibly released one day. I knew that by doing that, I would be publicly taking a position opposite from the one taken by the only remaining members of my nuclear family, who supported the sentence David was serving.

I took no pleasure in that fact; on the contrary, it was deeply painful. It was also a matter of faith and conscience. For years, I had been a prominent public supporter of keeping juveniles serving life without parole sentences locked up forever; it would have been cowardice not to be equally public about my reversal of position on the issue.

The hearing was to take place at the Illinois Capitol on March 7, 2013, just days after I had visited David Biro for the first time. I had no idea who the people testifying on the other side would be. I learned when I arrived that morning that one of them would be my mother. Others would be some of my dear friends: Dora Larson, whose daughter Victoria was lured to her grave by a juvenile on probation for another offense. Ron Holt, a highly respected police official whose only child was gunned down by a juvenile on a bus. Ron's son Blair died heroically, shielding a girl on the bus from the attack. My mother, Dora, and Ron would be there, literally on the other side of the aisle to speak against the bill. The prospect of that felt like a rock in the pit of my stomach. The daughter, as Jesus had promised, was set against her mother, both of us Christians believing that what we were doing was right. There is great pain in that moment of separation.

I reached out to my saints for help, and they gave it. One dear friend I turned to was the incomparable Susan Stabile, a writer, law professor, and Catholic spiritual director. I wrote to her shortly before the hearing, asking her to give me a mantra, something to carry with me into that hearing room. Susan wrote back: "From the prayer, the Anima Christi: Jesus, with you by my side, enough has been given. (Or, as it is phrased in Philippians, I can do all things through Christ, who strengthens me.)"

That prayer hovered around me all day as I walked the corridors of the Capitol: *Enough has been given.* It flooded my heart at the moment before the hearing began when I crossed the aisle to wrap my arms around my mother in a long, close hug. "You know, this is going to be all right," she said, looking at me with a smile. And in that moment it was.

Here is another lesson this journey has taught me: There is a cost, but there is also blessing. And the blessing is not just alongside the cost, but embedded within it. One of those verses of Scripture I began to understand as never before was from the Beatitudes in Jesus' Sermon on the Mount: "Blessed are you when people revile you and persecute you and utter all kinds of evil against you falsely on my account" (Matt. 5:11).

I was starting to grasp why that is a *blessing.* Doing the work that Jesus calls us to is transgressive; it is drawing outside the lines. It discomforts people. They disapprove. I started noticing in the Gospels that Jesus, throughout his public ministry, seemed to be followed around by a chorus of naysayers questioning everything he did. Why was he sitting down to eat with sinners and tax collectors? Why was he healing people on the Sabbath, in violation of the religious rules? Almost every one of his acts of mercy drew condemnation.

My "aha" moment happened one day as I was waiting for a case to be called in the courthouse where I work. A friend, the distinguished criminal lawyer Jed Stone, came over to talk. He told me, wincing slightly, as if in pain remembering it, that he had seen some bitter words written about me by a family member. I had not read them. He didn't tell me what they said. He merely asked what he could do. "Pray?" I suggested, with a rueful laugh.

As I headed back to my office, reflecting, this flashed into my mind: *Blessed are you when people revile you. . . .* I could not expect everyone to like what I was doing or praise me for it. If I truly was being obedient to Christ's call to follow him, coming under attack from some quarters wasn't just part of the deal; it meant I was doing something right. It was at the heart of the joy of that journey. The word for "blessed" in the Beatitudes, from which that verse comes, can also be translated this way: *Happy.*

Children taught me this. It happened on a clear morning in February, a day when snow was quietly piled up on the curbs, sparkling in the sunshine. I had been invited to Sacred Heart School in my hometown to speak to sixth-, seventh-, and eighth-graders about forgiveness and reconciliation. It would be one of the first times I would speak publicly about my visits with David Biro, and the first time ever to speak to a group so young. It was daunting—how would they react?

The private Catholic school starts each Wednesday morning with mass in the chapel, and I was invited to attend mass before the talk, if I wished. I did.

The chapel was lovely—airy and bright, lit by light filtered through the jewel-colored shards of the stained-glass windows. I entered late and sat alone in the back. The students were singing, their song of praise soaring up in the high-ceilinged sanctuary. The beauty and simplicity of the music washed over me; I found myself furtively wiping away tears. Children in red sweaters and uniform bottoms—plaid skirts for the girls and khakis for the boys—lined the pews.

When the moment came for the Lord's Prayer, the Our Father, the children did something I had never seen before: they made hand gestures along with the words of the prayer. Facing the altar at the front of the church, they accompanied each phrase of the prayer with graceful movements as they spoke the words aloud.

When we got to the words "Forgive us our trespasses, as we forgive those who trespass against us," the students did something that made me catch my breath: they stretched out their hands to one another, and clasped them, one hand to the left, the other to the right. The children formed a human chain stretching across the sanctuary, linked by hands and forgiveness.

It struck me: not all those children were friends. Maybe some had fought on the playground or gossiped about someone in a hallway. Maybe one student was nursing a wound from a hurt inflicted by the girl on her left, or another was smarting from a slight from the boy on his right. But they took one another's hands, each of them.

This is what it means, I thought as I watched the spectacle unfold. *"Love your enemies."* Hand in hand, you stand side by side on an equal plane with your enemy before God.

After mass, I gathered with about one hundred of those children in a rotunda in another part of the church and told my story. Some sat on the floor cross-legged, looking up as I spoke. Seeing their faces turned upward disarmed me; they reminded me of my own boys listening to a bedtime story.

I told of Nancy and Richard, who had lived in an apartment only a block away from the church as a happy young couple, of the murders, the arrest, the sentence, the change in me, my visits with David. The students' faces changed; you could see them pondering. The room was quiet as I finished; you could hear the slightest rustle of the wind on the snow outside.

The principal of the school, a lively, white-haired nun, came forward at the end to thank me. She turned to address the children: "Let's dismiss Ms. Bishop with a blessing."

A blessing? For me? I had never been given such a treasure before, especially not by angels in plaid skirts and khakis. The middle schoolers rose as a group and circled around me, raising their hands, palm down, in the air. I stood in their midst and bowed my head. The nun prayed aloud on behalf of all in the room, as they held their hands aloft, that I would go forth with God's blessing.

This is what led me to that moment: the story I had lived and told. The tears. The cost. Like every blessing, every grace, it was unearned. I had as much to atone for as anyone, and many of my scars were self-inflicted. Much of my life I have been a striver, the girl who wanted (and got) the best grades and the best job, who cringed when she failed. Part of that, perhaps, was the idea that I had to earn the blessing and affirmation of others and of God. In that moment, surrounded by children, I saw the deeper truth: grace is given, not earned, a function of being loved rather than of worldly accomplishment.

You fall from that bicycle and skid into the dirt, elbows skinned, or smack that water hard, and learn this: loving arms are there to lift you up and hold you fast. A voice is there to murmur words in your ear, tender and true, that you are brave and beloved. Then you get up and try again. Love bears you up. That changes everything.

Chapter 12

LEARNING FROM MY SAINTS

I KEPT MAKING THE LONG TREK TO SEE DAVID IN PRISON. I drove the plain, flat stretch of I-55 to see him every couple of months. We would write to each other in between. He would send me short stories he had written; I would send him favorite books to read.

On every visit, something would astonish me; some new epiphany would occur. One of the books I had given David was Louisa May Alcott's *Little Women*, the story of four sisters from a family named March, because it mirrors in part the way Nancy and I had grown up. I wanted him to understand the close bonds he had broken when he killed her. To me, my mother was the book's character Marmee, the warm, loving mother of a brood of girls. My older sister was Meg, the eldest of the March girls; I was Jo, the writer and wild-hearted tomboy of the family; and Nancy was Amy, the pretty one who loved clothes and parties. In *Little Women,* there is one more daughter, Beth, almost impossibly good and kind; she dies young of an illness. When Nancy was killed, I told David, it felt jarring. Nancy wasn't supposed to be Beth, who dies; she was supposed to be Amy, the one who marries and lives happily.

David Biro didn't see it that way. He said, you always describe Nancy as being all about love, and Beth was so loving. I think she was more like Beth, he added.

The truth of it took me aback; he was right. I had not seen it till then.

I learned more about David: he told me on a visit just before Christmas that his parents had never taken him to church as a child—not once. When he was around eight years old, he noticed that his friends' families were going to church. He wanted to go, too, and asked his mom to take him. She murmured something vague in response; nothing more ever came of it.

David wanted to learn about me, too. He was curious why I had become a public defender. How could I represent people like the ones he was in prison with, knowing the evil of which they were capable? I pointed out that his family had been able to afford to hire the skilled lawyer who represented him at trial; didn't poor defendants deserve the same level of representation? David was guilty, but he went to trial to make the state prove his guilt. My job, I told him, was to do the same, to test the evidence before the state can take the freedom of any man or woman, innocent or guilty.

David asked on another visit about my faith in God, whether it had a lot to do with what I did. I responded that God had everything to do with it. "If not for that, I wouldn't be here," I told him. "I would still be wishing you would stay in prison for the rest of your life."

Sometimes what I said to David seemed to perplex him. He could not understand, for example, why he should feel bad about having falsely accused his former friend of killing Nancy and Richard. Nobody believed me, David said, so what did it matter? "But they could have believed you!" I answered. "An innocent man could have done all this time you have done in prison, for a crime he didn't commit."

This work of reconciliation we were engaged in was new territory for me, an unexplored frontier, and I needed direction. There was so much I had to learn! I didn't even know what was fair to expect from David. I needed to educate myself, to read up and reach out to wiser heads than mine to help inform this seat-of-the-pants restorative justice I was doing.

My starting point was that term, "restorative justice"—what did it mean, anyway? Both as a lawyer and as a survivor of murder victims, I had heard about restorative justice, but found its definition elusive. People couldn't agree on whom it was even for. Some argue that the "restorative" part means working to restore the offender to society. Others contend that restorative means restoring the victims, trying to make them whole from their loss. Still others stake out a kind of middle ground, describing restorative justice as a process for both offenders and victims, bringing them together in an effort toward mutual healing.

The lawyer part of me turned to *Black's Law Dictionary*, which defines restorative justice this way: *An alternative delinquency sanction that focuses on repairing the harm done, meeting the victim's needs, and holding the offender responsible for his or her actions.*

Some articles I read described restorative justice as a voluntary truth-telling encounter among parties to a conflict, sharing stories and experiences. That sounded like what David Biro and I were doing. But our way wasn't the only way. Restorative justice can take a number of different forms: victim-offender meetings mediated by a third party, healing circles, truth commissions. The post-apartheid Truth and Reconciliation Commission in South Africa is perhaps the most famous example of restorative justice. One pioneering program in New York thrives on creativity; it made possible, for example, an encounter between the victim of an armed robbery and the perpetrator during which the victim was allowed to bring along his two young daughters. "Do you see these two girls?" the victim demanded of the man who had robbed him at gunpoint. "They are all I thought of when you put that gun in my face. How I would never see them again. How they would have to grow up without a father." The victim, powerless during the incident, felt powerful; the perpetrator was shaken to his core. He had children, too.

I looked in Scripture for passages about restoration and justice and found verses I had never noticed before:

> For thus says the Lord God: I myself will search for
> my sheep, and will seek them out. . . . I will seek the
> lost, and I will bring back the strayed, and I will bind

up the injured, and I will strengthen the weak. . . . I
will feed them with justice. (Ezek. 34:11, 16)

There is hope for your future, says the LORD; your
children shall come back to their own country. Indeed
I heard Ephraim pleading: "You disciplined me, and I
took the discipline; I was like a calf untrained. Bring
me back, let me come back, for you are the LORD my
God. For after I had turned away I repented; and after
I was discovered, I struck my thigh; I was ashamed,
and I was dismayed because I bore the disgrace of
my youth." Is Ephraim my dear son? Is he the child
I delight in? As often as I speak against him, I still
remember him. Therefore I am deeply moved for
him; I will surely have mercy on him, says the LORD.
(Jer. 31:17–20)

This story of shame, of judgment, of hope, of long-
ing to come home! The pleading, the plaintive cry:
Bring me back. Let me come back. I had heard it from my
clients, men and women locked away from all that was
dearest to them. The yearning is real, and strong.

The book of Jeremiah goes on, "See, I am the
LORD, the God of all flesh; is anything too hard for
me?" (Jer. 32: 27).

That was it, the heart of my search: *Is anything too hard
for God?* Is anyone beyond the forgiveness and redemption and purpose of God? Can we wipe our hands of
any human being, the way I had of David Biro?

For answers, I turned to my saints, people who
have labored in the fields of justice and faith—who
are, for me, a kind of true north. Our conversations
happened while I was sitting in kitchens as someone I
loved cooked me dinner, or walking arm in arm down a
hallway at a conference, or talking on a cell phone at an

airport gate. The wisdom I received! Gifts given freely, rich and unforgettable.

One of the most remarkable people I know is Bernardine Dohrn—mother, grandmother, law professor, open heart and intelligent mind, champion for the rights of children and women. Her concern for prisoners comes in part from her own time as a fugitive and as a prisoner (look up her name and Weather Underground, and see her metamorphosis from 1960s' activist to tenacious advocate for our most vulnerable citizens). She commands enormous respect from the legal community; she also wears a cheery red flower in her tousled hair every day.

Dohrn's groundbreaking Children and Family Justice Center at Northwestern University School of Law established restorative justice panels for youth all over Chicago, bringing together victims, perpetrators, and community volunteers. Bernardine invited me to dinner in her Hyde Park brownstone, near the University of Chicago and the home of President Obama. Bernardine's kitchen is a brick-walled, high-windowed, open space she moves about freely in, stirring carrot ginger soup and pulling plates and bowls off of wooden shelves. She described the restorative justice process as something at once profoundly healing and intensely pragmatic:

"One kid broke into a truck and stole a man's radio. The man was in a rage. He needed that truck to go to work every day. It had his building materials in it for his construction job. It took days for him to get his stuff out of the truck, get it fixed; that meant days of him not working. In the [restorative justice] panel, he heard the kid, fumblingly and inadequately, explain what he was doing and why. The man saw the kid's mother. He melted. He saw himself as a kid, the stupid things he did. He suggested to the panel that the kid work for him four Saturdays in a row. The idea is to give something back.

"With the panels, the idea is to face your community with what you did. People want to fix the problem. As the perpetrator, you are actually getting to fix something you broke."

Sitting at her kitchen table laden with cheese, bread, and olives, I asked Bernardine how the voices of victims are heard in this process. What she told me rang true:

"The adversarial system in the U.S. frequently leaves all parties to criminal litigation dissatisfied, because it is pretty much all win or all lose. For victims and perpetrators, the system itself has little or no room for either of their voices. The system colludes to make them far apart from each other, to a place where they're silenced.

"In restorative justice, the perpetrator's role is to listen to the victim. The victims' role is to tell their story. The community's job is to make sure the perpetrator hears the harm he has done and to decide how he should repair the harm."

Sister Helen Prejean, a formidable combination of moral compass, shrewd political instinct, bold witness, brave heart, and Louisiana charm, told me a story of restorative justice between two parents, the father of a murder victim and the mother of the killer:

"My hero is Lloyd Leblanc. I wrote about him in *Dead Man Walking.* People in his community were saying, if you really loved your loved one, how can you not want the ultimate punishment? You've sustained the ultimate loss. Lloyd told me, 'I tried to go there. I didn't like the way it made me feel.'

"The community was saying, who cares if the family of the perpetrator suffers? They should have raised him better.

"Lloyd told me, 'I like to be kind. It's who I am. I realized they killed our son, but I'm not going to let them kill me. I'm going to follow the way that Jesus laid out.'

"Early on, when the sheriff brought him to the morgue to identify his son, Lloyd, an excellent mechanic, thought, 'There is David's body. I can't fix this.' It was one of those chasms in life.

Right then, he said the Our Father, with the word "forgive," and knew that was the path he needed to go down.

"The word 'forgive' is 'for' to 'give.' Giving for whom? What is the giving? Lloyd helped me realize the first person you are giving is yourself, for yourself. 'I do this because this is who I am.' Forgiving enlarged his heart.

"He heard what Mrs. Sonnier [the mother of Patrick, one of his son's killers] was going through. He heard what was happening to her in the town, how she couldn't even go to the store. One day, she heard someone on her front porch, close to the time of the execution of Patrick. It was Lloyd, with a basket of fruit. He gave it to her and said, 'I'm a parent just like you. I don't hold you responsible for the death of our son. Call me if you need me.'"

Marietta Jaeger, mother of a murdered child and a death penalty opponent, shone her radiant light on this subject when she spoke at the Kairos conference. I took notes, writing down almost every word. Here are some of them:

"Forgiveness is not for wimps. It is hard work. It takes diligent discipline. When [the man who killed Jaeger's daughter] was arrested, the charges were kidnapping and murder, a capital offense. What was God's idea of justice? Jesus is the justice of God made flesh. When I look at him, I see someone not to hurt us or destroy us, but to heal us and help us. I came to see that God's idea of justice is not destruction, but restoration."

Another of my saints, Hulitt Gloer, professor, pastor, author, man of deep faith, spoke with me between his classes at Baylor's Truett Seminary in Waco, Texas. Hulitt, who cotaught at Baylor with Mark Osler, is a still, deep pool of wisdom. Hulitt said:

"All the justice that God calls for is restorative in nature. Jesus' life was all about redemption. Micah 6 says there is justice and mercy; they are two sides of the same coin. Our justice must seek the redemption of those being judged.

"Jesus' whole understanding of justice is justice predicated on forgiveness, on doing an act of redemption for the offending person because we want to see that person restored to a valuable life. That is not the world's way. But it is Jesus' way. What he said and did may not seem reasonable to you, but it is still true. Reason isn't the point. Love is the point."

I asked, But what about those who say of some people, what you did is so terrible that we should lock you away forever? Hulitt answered:

"Many of the things we are called to do as Christians just seem totally absurd to the world. Are you willing to believe that God can take a life that has done incredible harm to another person and redeem that life for good? If we really believe in that God, then cannot we also allow for that to happen?

"We put God in a box and say, that person is beyond the reach of God's redemptive power. No one is beyond the reach of God's power. There is nothing God wants to do more than change the lives of people. Are we not willing to let God do that work in people's lives? Or are there barriers we set up because we believe that person could never be of value to anybody?"

I caught Hank Shea, a lifelong Catholic and former federal prosecutor turned law professor, on the phone between flights. Shea teaches in Minnesota and Arizona. He brings the felons he helped send to prison to speak to his classes. The ex-prisoners tell the students cautionary tales: *Don't do what I did.*

Shea had made a name for himself in the U.S. Department of Justice as the guy who could bring down corrupt businessmen, bankers, and lawyers and garner millions of dollars in penalties in the process. Now he is harnessing the witness of those same people to convince future lawyers and businesspeople not to cut ethical corners. It helps not only the students; it also helps the people Shea prosecuted to do good, to see redemption come from their disgrace.

Underlying all this is Shea's Christian faith. "Faith has been and always will be central to my life," he told me. "It's my core—the way I've tried to live my life. It's been my rock; it's influenced everything I've done."

Susan Stabile, lawyer, teacher, author, and spiritual director, reflected on restorative justice as she chopped vegetables for dinner in her fragrant kitchen in Minnesota. A wood fire crackled nearby; winter snow blanketed the world outside. Susan grew up in a big Italian American family in New York; you can still hear the New York in her voice and taste the Italian in her magnificent cooking. She told me:

"Restorative justice is completely Christian. We recognize that we are all interrelated, interconnected. To me, at the end of the day, the banquet won't be any fun—it won't be complete—unless everyone is at the table. How do you bring people back to community? What happens when we put people in jail is we remove them from community. But do we get to make the judgment that these people are irredeemable?"

All of this lodged in my heart. The wise words worked within me. They carved out an opening, a new, uncharted path, one that I saw had to be my own. I could not shoehorn what David Biro and I were doing into a category; we would write our own definition of restorative justice, one visit, one letter, one epiphany at a time.

It could be that our struggle over restorative justice is this: Sometimes restoration has to come without justice—it has to be grace.

I'm a public defender. Many of my clients are guilty, but some are innocent. If I go to trial for an innocent defendant and he is acquitted, there is great justice in that. It's a moment of relief and joy when the words "not guilty" are spoken. My heart soars. Other times, though, a guilty client goes free when the state drops the charges, or a judge grants my motion to quash arrest and suppress evidence, or a jury votes to acquit. What happens then feels less like justice and more like mercy.

The term "restorative justice" may promise too much—that we can have both restoration and justice. Often, though, grace is necessary to get to restoration, and that can be a path that is harder and steeper and truer to the cross. Christ, after all, was killed unjustly, but offered us—his killers—grace even in that moment. Maybe, to follow him, it is restorative *mercy* we must seek.

Chapter 13

RESTORATION

WHAT'S NEXT FOR DAVID BIRO AND ME? HOW WILL IT turn out? The answer is, I don't know.

As of this writing, there are so many unknowns! Our visits: David and I see each other every couple of months, but I never know whether one day he will simply decide to take me off his visiting list and end the conversation. For most of his life, he has been a prisoner, and as a public defender, I represent prisoners every day who blindside me with the way they turn. Every letter I get, I half-expect to be an angry denouncement, and exhale in relief when it is not.

The sentence he is serving: Because the U.S. Supreme Court has declared mandatory life without parole sentences for juveniles to be unconstitutional,

David has filed a petition to be resentenced; the petition is pending in the same courtroom where he was tried for murder. I have no idea how that will turn out. Will the judge allow him to be resentenced? If she does resentence David, will it be to life in prison, or something less? Those are open questions.

I do know this, though: It doesn't matter that I don't know how it will turn out. That is up to God. Jesus' parable of the Sower tells me so:

> That same day Jesus went out of the house and sat beside the sea. Such great crowds gathered around him that he got into a boat and sat there, while the whole crowd stood on the beach. And he told them many things in parables, saying: "Listen! A sower went out to sow. And as he sowed, some seeds fell on the path, and the birds came and ate them up. Other seeds fell on rocky ground, where they did not have much soil, and they sprang up quickly, since they had no depth of soil. But when the sun rose, they were scorched; and since they had no root, they withered away. Other seeds fell among thorns, and the thorns grew up and choked them. Other seeds fell on good soil and brought forth grain, some a hundredfold, some sixty, some thirty." (Matt. 13:1–8)

The seeds are sprinkled; they may blow away or be choked by weeds, or they may grow. My part is to be obedient to God's call to truly forgive, to speak that word of love and grace. God is the one—not me—who can plant those seeds of love and help them take root and grow within a human heart. I cannot change the heart of a killer. But God can.

Many people—there is no shortage of them—are willing to write off the David Biros of the world. I was one of those people once. Here was our argument: Look at what he did! It's so evil, so depraved, that only a malignant heart could have concocted it. He is without feeling. Any remorse he might express later is only a sham. He will never change.

It is not true. I know this from my own transformation. God changed my heart. Why not the heart of David Biro? Why not the hearts of the thousands of people languishing in prison who have committed crimes for which we are willing to lock them up forever, without a second thought?

We set up David Biro and the others as objects of fear. Let them out, we say, and they may come after us. Our lives will be in danger. I wonder now, though, whether what we are truly afraid of is not that they will never get better, but that they might.

The Bible tells a story of radical change, of a violent, tormented man Jesus encounters who lived among the dead. He is not even given a name:

> He lived among the tombs; and no one could restrain him any more, even with a chain; for he had often been restrained with shackles and chains, but the chains he wrenched apart, and the shackles he broke in pieces; and no one had the strength to subdue him. Night and day among the tombs and on the mountains he was always howling and bruising himself with stones. (Mark 5:3–5)

Jesus casts out the man's affliction, the "demon." The townspeople rush to find out what happened. They arrive and see this: not the man they had regarded as a monster, but "the demoniac sitting there, clothed and in his right mind, the very man who had had the [demons], and they were afraid" (Mark 5:15).

They were afraid. Not happy, not rejoicing, as a shepherd rejoices over finding the one lost sheep he was looking for, or a woman rejoices over the lost coin she has found. People were *afraid.* Why? Because this person they regarded as such a threat was no longer so. He was calm, clothed, in his right mind.

The villagers ask Jesus to go. Leave, they tell him. They do not want power like that in their midst.

What kind of power could work that change in one human being? How can we believe in, trust in, a power that great? It is beyond anything we could ask or think. No wonder we doubt it for others. And yet . . . and yet, in our truest hearts, we yearn for it for ourselves. For transformation, for second chances, for understanding and forgiveness, for arms outstretched to welcome us.

When Jesus gets into his boat to leave the village, in the story I just told, the man he cured begs to go with him. Jesus says no; he has a radically different future in mind for this man.

"But Jesus refused, and said to him, 'Go home to your friends, and tell them how much the Lord has done for you, and what mercy he has shown you'" (Mark 5:19).

Go home. Tell of how you have been restored. Speak of mercy.

Mercy, restoration, coming home.

There is this moment when I am visiting David in prison. We have been talking, face to face, for hours. We have been leaning in, intently, straining to look through glass, to listen through a telephone receiver. We are tired, like children who need a loving hand to take ours, a wiser voice to tell us it is time to come away now and rest.

We get up from our chairs, on opposite sides of that glass. I go to the hallway outside the visiting area; a prison guard takes him out to that hallway to say good-bye to me. We shake hands; we look into each other's eyes. I tell him I will come again.

Then this happens: I leave alone. I walk past the waiting room—the linoleum floor, the water fountain, the signs, the vending machines, the other visitors listening for the names of their loved ones to be called.

I walk down a short pathway and through the door of the guardhouse. I take my small key to the locker out of my pocket and retrieve my belongings. I sign out on the sheet I was given at the start of the visit, say good-bye to the guards who signed me in. They buzz me out of the heavy front door. There is something reassuring about those sounds, the loud buzzing followed by the sound of the motor that moves the door. A signal of release. I breathe out. I step outside into the fresh air, and breathe in.

I turn left onto the long sidewalk leading to the parking lot. My eyes squint from the brightness of the sun. I look back at the heavy, gray-brown prison building on my left, which seems to follow me as I go. The guard in the watchtower watches over me as I step into the lot. I look up and think: *He knows who I am now, why*

I am here. That alone bears witness to mercy. My fingers fumble for the car key in my pocket.

I find it and put it into the ignition, and now that machinery hums to life and carries me away, across the prairie where my parents grew up, where one grandfather worked in a factory and another grandfather worked as a prosecutor, where fields seem to stretch out forever—a flat plain of freedom and grace where I am from, and David Biro is, too.

APPENDIX

RESOURCES ON FORGIVENESS, RECONCILIATION, AND RESTORATIVE JUSTICE

Websites

Restorative Justice International, www.restorativejustice international.com

Restorative Justice Online, a service of the Prison Fellowship International Centre for Justice and Reconciliation, www.restorativejustice.org

Real Justice: Restorative Responses to Crime and Wrong-doing, by International Institute for Restorative Practices, www.realjustice.org

NYC Justice Corps, nycjusticecorps.org

Books

Kraybill, Donald, Steven M. Nolt, and David L. Weaver-Zercher. *Amish Grace: How Forgiveness Transcended Tragedy*. Hoboken, NJ: John Wiley & Sons, 2010.

Larson, Catherine Claire. *As We Forgive: Stories of Reconciliation from Rwanda.* Grand Rapids: Zondervan, 2009.

O'Brien, J. Randall. *Set Free by Forgiveness: The Way to Peace and Healing.* Grand Rapids: Baker Books, 2005.

Osler, Mark. *Jesus on Death Row: The Trial of Jesus and American Capital Punishment.* Nashville: Abingdon Press, 2009.

Prejean, Sister Helen. *Dead Man Walking.* New York: Random House, 2007.

Stevenson, Bryan. *Just Mercy: A Story of Justice and Redemption.* New York: Spiegel & Grau, 2014.

Thompson, Marjorie J. *Forgiveness: A Lenten Study.* Louisville, KY: Westminster John Knox Press, 2014.

Wiesenthal, Simon, Harry J. Cargas, and Bonny V. Fetterman. *The Sunflower: On the Possibilities and Limits of Forgiveness.* New York: Schocken Books, 1998.

Zehr, Howard. *Changing Lenses: A New Focus for Crime and Justice.* Harrisonburg, VA: Herald Press, 1990.

Documentaries

Jackson, Lisa F. *Meeting with a Killer: One Family's Journey.* 2001. 44 min., 17 sec. www.utexas.edu/research/cswr/rji/mwak.html

Spiritual Roots of Restorative Justice. 2013. 24 min., 4 sec. www.youtube.com/watch?v=pLTlgDalDvk

Thakur, Shanti. *Circles* (Native American practices of restorative justice). National Film Board of Canada, 1997. 58 min. www.shantithakur.com/circles.html

Academic Centers

Center for Justice and Peacebuilding, Eastern Mennonite University, Harrisonburg, Virginia

Center for Peacemaking and Conflict Studies, Fresno Pacific University, Fresno, California

Center for Restorative Justice and Peacemaking, University of Minnesota, St. Paul

Centre for Restorative Justice, Simon Fraser University, Burnaby, British Columbia

Community Justice Institute, Florida Atlantic University, Boca Raton, Florida

International Institute for Restorative Practices, Bethlehem, Pennsylvania

Restorative Justice Programs

California

Victim Offender Reconciliation Program of the Central Valley, Inc.
Tim Nightingale, Executive Director
4882 E. Townsend Ave.
Fresno, CA 93727
559-455-9803

Indiana

Victim-Offender Reconciliation Program of the Center for Community Justice
Anne Lehman, Coordinator
121 S. Third St.
Elkhart, IN 46516
574-295-6149

Iowa

Polk County Attorney's Office–Restorative Justice Center
Teri Mundell, Program Coordinator
222 Fifth Ave.
Des Moines, IA 50309
515-286-3057

Texas

Victim Offender Mediation/Dialogue (VOM/D)
Victim Services Division
Texas Department of Criminal Justice

8712 Shoal Creek Blvd., Suite 265
Austin, TX 78757
800-848-4284
vsd.vomd@tdcj.texas.gov

Other Resources

Presbyterian Church (U.S.A.) Resolution on Restorative Justice, approved by the 214th General Assembly (2002), www.pcusa.org/site_media/media/uploads/acswp/pdf/restorative-justice.pdf

U.S. Catholic Bishops Statement, "Responsibility, Rehabilitation, and Restoration: A Catholic Perspective on Crime and Criminal Justice," November 2000, http://usccb.org/issues-and-action/human-life-and-dignity/criminal-justice-restorative-justice/crime-and-criminal-justice.cfm

United Methodist Church Mission Plan for Restorative Justice Ministries, 2012, www.umc.org/what-we-believe/mission-plan-for-restorative-justice-ministries